Keto Vegan Cookbook for Beginners

Text Copyright © Thomas Slow

All rights reserved. No part of this guide may be reproduced in any form without permission in writing from the publisher except in the case of brief quotations embodied in critical articles or reviews.

Legal & Disclaimer

The information contained in this book and its contents is not designed to replace or take the place of any form of medical or professional advice; and is not meant to replace the need for independent medical, financial, legal or other professional advice or services, as may be required. The content and information in this book have been provided for educational and entertainment purposes only.

The content and information contained in this book have been compiled from sources deemed reliable, and it is accurate to the best of the Author's knowledge, information, and belief. However, the author cannot guarantee its accuracy and validity and cannot be held liable for any errors and/or omissions. Further, changes are periodically made to this book as and when needed. Where appropriate and/or necessary, you must consult a professional (including but not limited to your doctor, attorney, financial advisor or such other professional advisor) before using any of the suggested remedies, techniques, or information in this book.

Upon using the contents and information contained in this book, you agree to hold harmless the Author from and against any damages, costs, and expenses, including any legal fees potentially resulting from the application of any of the information provided by this book. This disclaimer applies to any loss, damages or injury caused by the use and application, whether directly or indirectly, of any advice or information presented, whether for breach of contract, tort, negligence, personal injury, criminal intent, or under any other cause of action.

You agree to accept all risks of using the information presented inside this book.

You agree that by continuing to read this book, where appropriate and/or necessary, you shall consult a professional (including but not limited to your doctor, attorney, or financial advisor or such other advisor as needed) before using any of the suggested remedies, techniques, or information in this book.

Table of Contents

TABLE OF CONTENTS 3
INTRODUCTION 7
CHAPTER 1: VEGANISM 9
CHAPTER 2: KETOGENIC DIET 13
CHAPTER 3: KETO-VEGAN DIET 17
CHAPTER 4: BREAKFAST CHOICES 20

    STRAWBERRY PORRIDGE 20
    GINGERBREAD PORRIDGE 22
    OVERNIGHT STRAWBERRY CHEESECAKE PORRIDGE 24
    BLUEBERRY QUINOA PORRIDGE 25
    BLUEBERRY CHIA PUDDING 27
    ALMOND FLOUR MUFFINS 28
    BULLETPROOF TEA 30
    BULLETPROOF COFFEE 31
    COCONUT PANCAKES 32
    FLAXSEED PANCAKES 34
    BERRY AND NUT CEREAL 36
    PEANUT BUTTER FUDGY BROWNIES 37
    VANILLA GOLDEN TURMERIC CEREAL 40
    FUDGE OATMEAL 42
    RASPBERRY ALMOND SMOOTHIE 44
    VANILLA OVERNIGHT OATS 45
    CINNAMON OVERNIGHT OATS 46
    PUMPKIN SPICE OVERNIGHT OATS 47
    SMOOTHIE BOWL 48
    EGGY SURPRISE SCRAMBLE 50
    BAGELS 52
    CINNAMON ROLL MUFFINS 54

CHAPTER 5: LUNCH & DINNER FAVORITES 56

    MUSHROOM STEAK 56
    SPICY GRILLED TOFU STEAK 59
    PIQUILLO SALSA VERDE STEAK 61
    BUTTERNUT SQUASH STEAK 63
    CAULIFLOWER STEAK KICKING CORN 65
    PISTACHIO WATERMELON STEAK 67
    BBQ RIBS 68
    SPICY VEGGIE STEAKS WITH VEGGIES 72

Tofu Seitan	75
Stuffed Zucchini	77
Roasted Butternut Squash With Chimichurri	79
Eggplant Pizza	82
Green Avocado Carbonara	84
Curried Tofu	86
Sesame Tofu and Eggplant	88
Tempeh Coconut Curry	90
Tempeh Tikka Masala	93
Caprice Casserole	95
Cheesy Brussel Sprout Bake	97
Tofu Noodle Bowl	100
Cashew Siam Salad	102
Cucumber Edamame Salad	104
Caesar Vegan Salad	106
Mushroom Lettuce Wraps	109

CHAPTER 6: SIDE DISHES & SNACKS 111

Mixed Seed Crackers	111
Crispy Squash Chips	113
Paprika Nuts	115
Basil Zoodles and Olives	117
Roasted Beetroot Noodles	119
Turnip Fries	120
Lime and Chili Carrots Noodles	122
Pesto Zucchini Noodles	123
Cabbage Slaw	124
Zucchini Chips	126
Peanut Tofu Wrap	127
Cinnamon Granola	129
Chocolate Granola	131
Radish Chips	133
Asparagus Fries	134

CHAPTER 7: SAUCES & DIPS 136

Keto-Vegan Ketchup	136
Avocado Hummus	138
Guacamole	139
Keto-Vegan Mayo	141
Peanut Sauce	142
Pistachio Dip	143
Smokey Tomato Jam	145
Tasty Ranch Dressing/Dip	147

CHAPTER 8: SOUPS 148
- Goulash Soup 148
- Celery Dill Soup 150
- Broccoli Fennel Soup 152
- Broccoli and Cauliflower Soup 154
- Keto-Vegan Chili 156
- Creamy Avocado Soup 158
- Red Onion Soup 159
- Thai Pumpkin Soup 161
- Zucchini Basil Soup 162

CHAPTER 9: SMOOTHIES 164
- Chocolate Smoothie 164
- Chocolate Mint Smoothie 166
- Cinnamon Roll Smoothie 167
- Coconut Smoothie 168
- Maca Almond Smoothie 169
- Blueberry Smoothie 170
- Nutty Protein Shake 172
- Cinnamon Pear Smoothie 173
- Vanilla Milkshake 174
- Raspberry Protein Shake 175
- Raspberry Almond Smoothie 176

CHAPTER 10: DESSERTS 177
- Keto Chocolate Brownies 177
- Chocolate Fat Bomb 179
- Vanilla Cheesecake 180
- Chocolate Mousse 182
- Avocado Chocolate Mousse 184
- Coconut Fat Bombs 185
- Coconut Cupcakes 186
- Pumpkin Truffles 188
- Raspberry Truffles 190
- Strawberry Ice Cream 192
- Pistachio Gelato 194
- Chocolate Chip Ice Cream 195
- Cinnamon Vanilla Bites 197
- Berry Bites 199
- Coconut Chocolate Balls 200
- Espresso Cups 202

CONCLUSION 203

INDEX FOR THE RECIPES **205**

Introduction

Congratulations on purchasing your copy of the *Keto-Vegan Cookbook for Beginners*. I'm thrilled to help guide you in this adventure in improving your health. You are well on your way to discovering many great recipes to delight your taste buds.

You will find recipes for all types of tastes within these pages; each recipe will provide you with estimated cooking time, serving size, and nutritional values. I have worked very hard to take a lot of the guesswork out so that you can simply cook and enjoy.

I wrote this cookbook because there was a gap that needed to be filled: there are many vegan and keto options, but either of them did not make me feel that I'm eating according to my goals. I spent so much time making substitutions to recipes, researching what to use in place of certain ingredients, and re-figuring the nutritional facts that it just made sense to develop an easy guide for all our Keto-Vegan friends.

If you are tired of starting a recipe only to find that you need to make adjustments or change ingredients, then this is the book for you. I have worked tirelessly to ensure every recipe meets my high standards of being a Keto-Vegan.

There are plenty of cookbooks on the Keto or Vegan diet, so thanks again for choosing this one! Every effort was made to ensure that it is full of as much useful information as possible.

Chapter 1: Veganism

Veganism began in 1944 when a little group of vegetarians broke away to create the Vegan society. It was their choice not to consume any product that came from any animal. Some choose a vegan lifestyle for ethical reasons, such as the belief that all animal life is valuable, and they work to limit the exploitation of animals as much as possible. Some vegans choose this lifestyle for health reasons and others for environmental reasons.

When eating a vegan diet, these are some foods to avoid:

- Honey
- Fish
- Dairy
- Chicken
- Shellfish

- Meat

On the flip side of that, vegans still enjoy many of the normal fan favorites, such as bean burritos, veggie burgers, pizza, smoothies, and chips just with a twist. Vegans typically swap out those meat-based options with things like the following:

- Seeds
- Nuts
- Tempeh
- Seitan
- Tofu
- Lentils
- Beans

Milk products are also replaced with plant-based milk and honey with plant sweeteners.

If you are living a vegan lifestyle, it is important to ensure that your body is still getting all the vitamins and minerals it needs. There are seven basic supplements I suggest you include when choosing this lifestyle. Always consult your nutritionist or doctor if you have questions.

- Vitamin B12 – Yes, you can get b12 from some plant-based options; however, scientists believe that vegans are at a higher risk of b12 deficiency. Too little b12 can lead to anemia. The daily recommended dosage is 2.4 mcg for adults.

- Vitamin D – this is the vitamin that helps you to absorb calcium and phosphorus in the gut. Vitamin D also has influence over many other processes, such as muscle recovery, memory, mood, and immune function. Consider taking a vitamin D2 or D3 supplement daily.

- Long-Chain Omega-3s – These are your fatty acids; they are important to the structural role for your eyes and brain. The recommended dose is to take a supplement containing EPA and DHA of 200 to 300 mg.

- Iodine – This is crucial for the function of your metabolism and the health of your thyroid. The recommended dosage for an adult is 150 mcg of iodine.

- Iron – This is essential for helping the body create new red blood cells and DNA, as well as carry oxygen into the blood. Low levels of iron can also result in fatigue. The recommended dosage is 8 milligrams for a male per day and 18 milligrams for a woman per day.

- Calcium – This mineral is essential for healthy teeth and bones, as well as the health of the heart. The recommended dosage amount is 1,000 mg per day.

- Zinc – This mineral is responsible for the repair of body cells, immune function, and metabolism. Insufficient zinc levels can result in diarrhea, hair loss, and developmental problems. The recommended dosage for zinc is 8 mg per day.

With all this being said, you can achieve many of these vitamins and nutrients through your plant-based diet. However, it is important to consider the use of supplements to offset the gaps between diet and body needs. Always remember to consult your health care professional.

Chapter 2: Ketogenic Diet

Keto is short for Ketogenic. A "Ketogenic Diet" is basically a low-carb diet. Through this diet, you are focusing your calorie intake on protein while reducing your calorie intake from fat and carbohydrates. There are specific food types that the body can digest easier than others. These would include things like sugar, soda, sweets, and white bread. Your body actually uses these sugary sources as fuel. Think of it like using regular gas in your car. It works great; however, when you put premium fuel, you often get a better mile per gallon ratio. The human body works the same way; the better fuel you give it, the more efficient it works.

When starting out with keto, it can take three to four days before the body has "burned" off the sugary fuel. To get to that point, you will want to focus on eating 50 grams of carbs or less per day. Once that sugar fuel is gone, the body will then begin to break down protein and fat for energy. Some begin to see weight loss right away. This process is called ketosis, which is the body's natural way of creating fuel through ketones when there are not enough carbs to burn for energy.

The keto lifestyle is typically a short-term diet with focus on weight loss. Those living on a keto lifestyle have seen significant increase in weight loss compared to the other diets during the initial months. However, weight loss is not the only reason people are living on a keto lifestyle. There have been some research studies conducted claiming that keto may help people with other medical conditions, such as diabetes, heart disease, and even acne. Be sure to consult a doctor if you have any serious medical condition before starting the keto diet.

Those on the keto diet must avoid these types of food:

- Grains rice
- Low-fat dairy
- Sugars
- Starchy vegetables like potatoes, corn
- Trans fats
- Alcohol

On the other side, keto dieters enjoy:

- Vegetables like tomatoes, eggplants, asparagus, leafy greens, cucumber, Bell pepper
- Chicken, turkey venison, beef, seafood, eggs, natural cheese, whole milk ricotta cheese
- Oils, flaxseed, chia seed, pumpkin seed, sesame seed, nuts, and no-sugar kinds of butter.

Like the vegan diet, the ketogenic diet may be lacking on some minerals and vitamins, so taking supplements may be the best approach. Some of these are also listed under the vegan diet. Here are at least five supplements recommended when on a keto diet:

- Magnesium – This helps with your cellular functions, regulates the immune system, and strengthens the muscles and nerves. The recommended dosage is 310 mg.

- Calcium – The recommended dosage is also 1,000 mg per day.

- Iron – Take 8 milligrams a fay if you are a male and 18 milligrams if you are a woman.

- Vitamin D – Take vitamin D2 or D3, one tablet a day.

- Fiber – Fiber helps to keep your gut healthy and the GI tract running smooth. It is recommended to discuss with your health care professional for the appropriate dosage based on your body's needs.

You can get many of the vitamins and nutrients that your body needs from the keto diet. However, as we have mentioned earlier, it would still be better to fill the gaps that this lifestyle may create.

Chapter 3: Keto-Vegan Diet

The keto-vegan lifestyle is one of the most restrictive lifestyles that suggest a very specific diet. However, it is possible to follow. In this lifestyle, you are focusing on a diet that is free of food products derived from animals. The diet is also low in carbohydrates. One of the key factors to success in this lifestyle is to eat not more than 5% of calories from carbohydrates. That would be approximately 50 grams of carbs in one day. However, many recommend staying at the lower end of 35 grams per day. Additionally, it is important to receive 70% of daily calories from plant-based fats and 25% from plant-based proteins.

Those on the keto-vegan diet should avoid these types of food:

- Grains, wheat, corn, rice
- Sugars – honey

- Fruit – apples, bananas
- Starches – potato, yams

On the other hand, keto dieters may enjoy the following:

- Vegan meats
- Mushrooms
- Leafy greens – kale, spinach
- Above-ground vegetables – cauliflower, zucchini, broccoli
- Seeds and nuts
- Avocados
- Berries
- Sea vegetables
- Sweeteners – stevia, monk fruit

Many studies have shown that a keto-vegan lifestyle provides health benefits. These benefits include lowering the risk of heart disease, greater mental health, improved vision, better stomach and gut health, and improved sleep. As always, make sure you are working with your healthcare professional to ensure you are getting all the vitamins and minerals that your body needs.

One thing is for sure; it is easier than before to live on a keto-vegan lifestyle with all the healthy food choices out there. There is also an abundance of alternatives for dairy and eggs that can help keep you on track with the keto portion of your life. The following chapters present the different recipes you can try while on the vegan-keto diet.

Chapter 4: Breakfast Choices

You can make a wide-range of breakfast treats, from tasty muffins to smoothies, to get your day kick-started in the right way.

Strawberry Porridge

Total Prep & Cooking Time: 9 min.

Yields: 2 Servings

Nutrition Facts: Calories: 374 | Proteins: 11 g | Carbohydrates: 9 g | Fats: 33 g

Ingredients

1/3 c. coconut milk, full-fat canned

½ c. water

1 tbsp. coconut flour

¼ c. hemp seeds

½ c. flacked unsweetened coconut

2 strawberries sliced

½ tbs. ground cinnamon

1 t. vanilla

1-2 teaspoons sweetener of your choice.

Follow these simple steps:

1. Add milk, water, coconut, coconut flour, & hemp seed to a pan for cooking on the stove.
2. In this pan, allow these ingredients to a come to a boil for approximately 2 minutes, simmering until thick.
3. Add cinnamon & vanilla and combine until well-mixed and put in a heat-resistant bowl.
4. Slice the strawberries and place on top of the porridge and sprinkle the sweetener of your choice across the top.
5. Enjoy with additional milk as needed.

Gingerbread Porridge

Total Prep & Cooking Time: 9 min.

Yields: 2 Servings

Nutrition Facts: Calories: 374 | Proteins: 11 g | Carbohydrates: 9 g | Fats: 33 g

Ingredients

1/3 c. coconut milk, full-fat, canned

½ c. water

1 tbsp. coconut flour

¼ c. hemp seeds

½ c. flacked unsweetened coconut

1 ½ t. ground ginger

1 t. of the following:
- ground cloves
- ground nutmeg
- vanilla

½ tbsp. ground cinnamon

1-2 teaspoons sweetener of your choice

Optional Toppings

Almond butter, chopped walnuts/pecans, cranberries

Follow these simple steps:

1. In a medium saucepan, add the milk, water, coconut, coconut flour, & hemp seed.
2. Bring these ingredients to a boil, allowing to simmer 2 minutes or until thickened.
3. Add cinnamon, vanilla ginger, cloves, nutmeg, and combine until well-mixed and put in a heat-resistant bowl.
4. Sprinkle sweetener and any optional toppings of your choice across the top.
5. Mix and enjoy with additional milk as needed.

Overnight Strawberry Cheesecake Porridge

Total Prep & Cooking Time: 10 min.

Yields: 1 Servings

Nutrition Facts: Calories: 275 | Proteins: 8 g | Carbohydrates: 16 g | Fats: 17 g

Ingredients

¼ c. fresh strawberries

½ c. coconut milk

2 tbsp. of the following:
- coconut yogurt
- ground flaxseed
- chia seeds
- sweetener of your choice

1 tbsp. of the following:
- almond flour
- shredded unsweetened coconut

Follow these simple steps:

1. Mix almond flour, unsweetened coconut, sweetener, chia seed, and flaxseed in a shallow bowl.
2. Next, pour ¼ cup of the coconut milk with dry contents and combine well.
3. Refrigerate overnight.

4. Before serving, add the remaining milk until the mixture becomes thick and creamy.
5. Layer the yogurt and strawberries on top.
6. Mix and enjoy.

Blueberry Quinoa Porridge

Total Prep & Cooking Time: 20 min.

Yields: 2 Servings

Nutrition Facts: Calories: 374 | Proteins: 11 g | Carbohydrates: 9 g | Fats: 33 g

Ingredients

1 c. blueberries

1/8 t. cinnamon

¼ t. vanilla

1 tbsp. sweetener of your choice

2 c. almond milk

1 c. uncooked quinoa

Optional Toppings

Chia seeds, hemp seeds, hazelnuts

Follow these simple steps:

1. In a saucepan, add milk and quinoa.

2. Heat milk and quinoa at low heat for roughly 10 minutes, stirring to prevent scorching.
3. Slowly combine vanilla, cinnamon, and sugar and cook for 5 minutes or when the quinoa soft.
4. Take away from the heat and place in serving bowls.
5. Top with blueberries and sprinkle sweetener of your choice across the top.
6. Mix and enjoy.

Blueberry Chia Pudding

Total Prep & Cooking Time: 8 hours 10 min.

Yields: 3 Servings

Nutrition Facts: Calories: 374 | Proteins: 11 g | Carbohydrates: 9 g | Fats: 33 g

Ingredients

1/8 t. cinnamon

½ t. vanilla

2 c. almond milk, unsweetened

1 tbsp. maple syrup

1/3 c. blueberries

6 tbsp. chia seeds, fresh

Follow these simple steps:

1. Combine the chia seeds, blueberries, syrup, milk, vanilla, and cinnamon into a blender, blending into a silky consistency.
2. Separate mixture into 3 glasses or ramekins.
3. Chill overnight or until set, approximately 8 hours.
4. Enjoy it chilled.

Pro Tip:

Using frozen blueberries will allow the mixture to have a little more texture

Almond Flour Muffins

Total Prep & Cooking Time: 10 min.

Yields: 4 regular size Muffins or 14 Mini Muffins Servings

Nutrition Facts: Calories: 217 | Proteins: 11 g | Carbohydrates: 9 g | Fats: 33 g

Ingredients

¼ t. salt

½ tbsp. baking powder

1 flax egg

¼ c. almond milk

1 tbsp. stevia (or your sweetener of choice)

1 c. almond flour

Olive oil for greasing muffin pan.

Optional add-in

Crushed, walnuts, blueberries, sugar-free chocolate chips

Follow these simple steps:

1. Set the oven to preheat at 350.
2. Grease the muffin pan with olive oil.
3. Combine baking powder, stevia, salt, and almond flour in a mixing bowl. Mix completely.
4. Slowly add the flax egg and almond milk and mix well
5. If adding any add-ins, add them at this point (crushed walnuts, blueberries, chocolate chips).
6. Using a ¼ c. measuring cup, fill each muffin tin approximately 2/3 full.
7. Carefully slide into the oven and cook for 10 minutes (mini size) or 15 minutes (regular size).
8. Take it from oven and place in a cool area to allow muffins to cool while still in the tin for about 10 minutes. Then, carefully remove the muffins using a knife to loosen them from the sides of the tin.

Bulletproof Tea

Total Prep & Cooking Time: 2 min.

Yields: 1 Serving

Nutrition Facts: Calories: 151 | Proteins: 0 g | Carbohydrates: 1 g | Fats: 17 g

Ingredients

1/8 t. ground cinnamon

1 tbsp. of the following:
- coconut milk
- coconut oil

1-2 t. black tea

8 oz. boiling water

Sweetener of your choice

Follow these simple steps:

1. Begin by boiling 8 oz of water.
2. Then add the black tea to steep according to your package directions.
3. Once the tea is done steeping, pour it into a blender then add coconut oil, coconut milk, cinnamon, and a sweetener of your choice.
4. Blend approximately 30 seconds or until smooth.
5. Pour into a cup and enjoy.

Bulletproof Coffee

Total Prep & Cooking Time: 3 min.

Yields: 2 Serving

Nutrition Facts: Calories: 354 | Proteins: 4.4 g | Carbohydrates: 4.7 g | Fats: 37.2 g

Ingredients

2 c. strong coffee

¼ cup almond milk, unsweetened

2 tbsp. coconut oil, extra virgin

1 oz. raw cacao butter

1 1/2 tbsp. almond butter

Follow these simple steps:

1. In a microwave-safe pitcher, heat cacao butter, coconut oil, and almond butter until melted; this may take approximately 20 seconds.
2. Add the almond milk slowly and stir.
3. Microwave an additional 30 seconds.
4. Remove from the microwave and add coffee. Blend with a handheld froth machine or blender until creamy.
5. Pour into a cup and enjoy.

Coconut Pancakes

Total Prep & Cooking Time: 10 min.

Yields: 4 Serving

Nutrition Facts: Calories: 491 | Proteins: 11 g | Carbohydrates: 41.9 g | Fats: 33 g

Ingredients

1 t. cinnamon

1 ½ c. coconut milk

1/3 c. coconut flour

1 big banana

1 c. quinoa flakes

1 serving liquid stevia

1 t. baking powder

2/3 c. almond flour

Follow these simple steps:

1. Combine in a big glass bowl the baking powder with both types of flour. Mix well.
2. In the blender, add stevia, quinoa flakes, banana, and cinnamon until well-mixed.
3. Add big bowl to the blender and begin adding coconut milk ½ cup at a time. If the mixture is thick, add additional milk; if it's not thin enough, add some more almond flour. Allow the batter to rest for about 5 minutes.
4. Warm a big flat pan to medium heat.
5. Using a ¼ cup measuring cup, scoop the batter from the blender. Pour in the skillet, covering to cook for 2 minutes or when bubbles begin to form. Flip and repeat.
6. Enjoy warm.

Flaxseed Pancakes

Total Prep & Cooking Time: 10 min.

Yields: 4 Serving

Nutrition Facts: Calories: 239 | Proteins: 12.6 g | Carbohydrates: 8.7 g | Fats: 18.9 g

Ingredients

¼ t of the following:
- vanilla
- baking soda

1 t. apple cider vinegar

1 flax egg

¼ c. ground golden flaxseed meal

1 tbsp. almond milk

Dash of cinnamon & nutmeg

Pinch of sea salt

Follow these simple steps:

1. Incorporate all of the above in a big glass bowl and mix. The batter should be a thicker mixture and sticky. If it doesn't spread well in the pan, add more milk.
2. Warm a flat pan or griddle to medium heat. Using olive oil, grease the pan to prevent the pancakes from sticking.

3. Using a spoon, scoop the batter from the bowl and form 2-3 pancakes in your pan. Use the spoon to help flatten out the batter.
4. Cook 2 minutes or until bubbles are forming. Flip and repeat; be sure to keep a close eye on these, so they do not burn.
5. Enjoy warm.

Berry and Nut Cereal

Total Prep & Cooking Time: 15 min.

Yields: 2 Serving

Nutrition Facts: Calories: 776 | Proteins: 10.8 g | Carbohydrates: 27.7 g | Fats: 73.3 g

Ingredients

1/3 c. of the following:
- strawberries
- blueberries
- toasted flaxseed
- crushed walnut pieces

2 c. almond milk

½ c. shredded unsweetened coconut

Pinch of salt

Follow these simple steps:

1. In a saucepan, toast nuts and salt over low to medium heat; cook for approximately 2 minutes.
2. Add shredded coconut and stir constantly to prevent burning; do this for about 1 minute.
3. Once toasted, add almond milk and stir to combine.
4. Pull from the heat and divide into 2 bowls.
5. Divide the strawberries and blueberries between bowls

6. Sprinkle with a sweetener of your choice.
7. Enjoy warm.

Peanut Butter Fudgy Brownies

Total Prep & Cooking Time: 20 min.

Yields: 9 Serving

Nutrition Facts: Calories: 321 | Proteins: 9.6 g | Carbohydrates: 30.1 g | Fats: 22.5 g

Ingredients

2/3 c. chocolate chips

¾ c. of the following:
- brown sugar
- peanut butter
- almond milk

½ t. of each:

- salt
- baking powder

¼ c. cacao powder

1 t. vanilla

1 c. almond flour

2 tbsp. ground flax

5 tbsp. water

Follow these simple steps:

1. Begin by bringing the oven temperature to 350.
2. While the oven is preheating, combine in a bowl the ground flax and water, allowing these to sit for approximately 5 minutes to thicken.
3. Next, in a big mixing bowl, add salt, baking powder, cacao powder, and almond flour.
4. In the center of the mixture, form a well and add in the thickened flax water mixture, vanilla, coconut sugar, peanut butter, and milk.
5. Stir until the mixture forms a nice thick batter.
6. Next, fold in the chocolate chips.
7. In a 9x9 greased baking dish, pour the batter using a spatula to even it out.
8. On top, add 5 dollops of peanut butter, then using a knife, swirl the peanut butter into the brownie batter.

9. Place brownies in the preheated oven, baking for 20 minutes. Allow the brownies to reduce in temperature in the pan for 10 minutes.
10. After this, you can place the yummy treats on a cooling rack. Slice and enjoy!

Vanilla Golden Turmeric Cereal

Total Prep & Cooking Time: 55 min.

Yields: 2 Serving

Nutrition Facts: Calories: 585 | Proteins: 9.4 g | Carbohydrates: 84.5 g | Fats: 21.6 g

Ingredients

1 c. almond milk unsweetened vanilla silk

3 tbsp. coconut oil melted

¼ t. ground cloves

½ t. ginger

1 tbsp. of the following:
- turmeric
- cinnamon
- vanilla

6 tbsp. maple syrup

1 t. Himalayan salt

3 tbsp. ground flaxseed

3 c. quinoa flakes

Follow these simple steps:

1. Begin by bringing the oven temperature to 350.
2. Combine the cloves, ginger, turmeric, cinnamon, vanilla, syrup, salt flax, and quinoa flakes in a big mixing bowl.

3. Move to a cookie sheet in an even layer, approximately ½ inch thick. Place the mixture in the oven, baking for 40 minutes. Every 10 minutes, stir to get even cooking and prevent the edges from burning.
4. Let it cool completely.
5. Add them to the bowls and pour almond milk over the top.
6. Enjoy.

Fudge Oatmeal

Total Prep & Cooking Time: 5 min.

Yields: 1 Serving

Nutrition Facts: Calories: 262 | Proteins: 9 g | Carbohydrates: 14 g | Fats: 18 g

Ingredients

½ t. vanilla

2 tbsp. chocolate chips

2 t. cocoa powder

2 tbsp. of the following:
- ground flaxseed
- chia seed
- unsweetened shredded coconut
- sweetener of your choice

½ c. hot water

¾ c. coconut milk

Follow these simple steps:

1. Add ground flaxseed, chia seed, shredded coconut, and sweetener of your choice to a bowl and mix well.
2. Pour ½ cup of hot water into the dry ingredients and mix well. It will be thick.
3. Add ½ cup coconut milk to make a creamy oatmeal base.

4. Next, add ¼ cup milk, vanilla, chocolate chips, and cocoa powder.
5. Heat over the stovetop or in the microwave until the chocolate chips have melted.
6. Top with the reaming chocolate chips and enjoy.
7. Enjoy.

Raspberry Almond Smoothie

Total Prep & Cooking Time: 5 min.

Yields: 1 Serving

Nutrition Facts: Calories: 156 | Proteins: 2.8 g | Carbohydrates: 26.6 g | Fats: 5.4 g

Ingredients

3 t. maple syrup

½ c. raspberry

2 c. almond milk unsweetened vanilla silk

Follow these simple steps:

1. Combine in a blender the almond milk, raspberries, and syrup and blend for 3 minutes or until smooth. If it seems too dense, i.e., it's difficult to drink, add an additional ¼ cup of milk.

2. Enjoy.

Vanilla Overnight Oats

Total Prep & Cooking Time: 5 min.

Yields: 1 Serving

Nutrition Facts: Calories: 132 | Proteins: 6.5 g | Carbohydrates: 4.9 g | Fats: 1 g

Ingredients

½ t. vanilla

3 to 4 drops liquid stevia

1 tbsp. chia seed

½ c. hemp hearts

2/3 c. almond milk unsweetened vanilla silk

Follow these simple steps:

1. Add hemp hearts, chia seed, stevia, vanilla, and ½ the milk to a bowl; mix it until well-combined.
2. Cover and refrigerate overnight or for a minimum of 8 hours.
3. Remove from the fridge, divide into 2 bowls, and enjoy with a splash of milk.

Cinnamon Overnight Oats

Total Prep & Cooking Time: 5 min.

Yields: 1 Serving

Nutrition Facts: Calories: 132 | Proteins: 6.5 g | Carbohydrates: 4.9 g | Fats: 1 g

Ingredients

½ t. vanilla

½ tbsp. cinnamon

3 to 4 drops liquid stevia

1 tbsp. chia seed

½ c. hemp hearts

2/3 c. almond milk unsweetened vanilla silk

Follow these simple steps:

1. Add hemp hearts, chia seed, stevia, cinnamon, vanilla, and ½ the milk to a bowl; mix the ingredients until well-combined.
2. Cover and refrigerate overnight or for 8 hours.
3. When ready for serving, take it out of the fridge, scoop some into a bowl, and enjoy with the remaining milk.

Pumpkin Spice Overnight Oats

Total Prep & Cooking Time: 5 min.

Yields: 1 Serving

Nutrition Facts: Calories: 132 | Proteins: 6.5 g | Carbohydrates: 4.9 g | Fats: 1 g

Ingredients

½ t. vanilla

¾ t. pumpkin spice

3 to 4 drops liquid stevia

1 tbsp. chia seed

2 tbsp. canned pumpkin puree

½ c. hemp hearts

1/3 c. of the following:

- brewed coffee
- almond milk unsweetened vanilla silk

Follow these simple steps:

1. In a bowl with a lid, add all the ingredients, mixing until well-combined.
2. Cover and refrigerate overnight or 8 hours.
3. Remove from the fridge and add additional milk until the oats reach your desired consistency.
4. Divide into 2 bowls and enjoy.

Smoothie Bowl

Total Prep & Cooking Time: 15 min.

Yields: 2 Serving

Nutrition Facts: Calories: 253 | Proteins: 6.5 g | Carbohydrates: 4.9 g | Fats: 1 g

Ingredients

1 t. ground cinnamon

3 tbsp. hemp hearts

2 tbsp. almond butter

1 c. of the following:
- vanilla unsweetened almond milk
- frozen blueberries
- frozen spinach

½ c. of the following:
- frozen zucchini
- frozen cauliflower

Follow these simple steps:

1. Throw the cauliflower, zucchini, spinach, blueberries, milk, almond butter, hemp hearts, and cinnamon into a high-speed blender. Ensure the frozen ingredients are closest to the blades.
2. Blend until it's a smooth, creamy consistency.
3. Divide into 2 bowls and enjoy.

Eggy Surprise Scramble

Total Prep & Cooking Time: 10 min.

Yields: 2 Serving

Nutrition Facts: Calories: 206 | Proteins: 20.3 g | Carbohydrates: 4 g | Fats: 13.1 g

Ingredients

1/3 c. soy milk

¼ t. of the following:

- onion powder
- black salt (Kala Namak)

½ t. of the following:

- garlic powder
- paprika
- turmeric

1 t. Dijon mustard

1 tbsp. vegan butter

2 tbsp. nutritional yeast

8oz extra firm tofu

Optional ingredients

- black pepper
- chives

- fried Tomatoes
- sliced Avocado

Follow these simple steps:

1. With a fork, chop the tofu into nice big chunks.
2. Combine in the mixing bowl garlic powder, onion powder, black pepper, salt, mustard, paprika, yeast, and turmeric. Once mixed well, whisk in the soy milk to create a sauce.
3. Warm over a medium heat a skillet, adding butter and stirring to melt.
4. Next, apply the tofu and fry until a light golden color; be careful not to over-scramble the tofu.
5. Add the sauce mixture to the tofu and fry until the sauce has been mostly absorbed by the tofu.
6. Remove it from skillet and transfer to a plate; top it with optional ingredients and enjoy.

Bagels

Total Prep & Cooking Time: 50 min.

Yields: 6 Serving

Nutrition Facts: Calories: 209 | Proteins: 6.6 g | Carbohydrates: 2 g | Fats: 16.4 g

Ingredients

Pinch of salt

1 t. baking powder

¼ c. psyllium husks

½ c of the following:
- tahini
- ground flaxseed

1 c. water

Optional ingredients

Almond butter, fresh fruit

Follow these simple steps:

1. Set the oven to 375 heat setting.
2. In a mixing bowl medium in size, add salt, flaxseed, baking powder, and psyllium husk.
3. Whisk until well-combined.
4. In a little bowl, add water and tahini and whisk until combined.

5. Add the wet ingredients in the small bowl to the medium bowl and knead until the dough is well-worked and has a uniform consistency.
6. Using your hands, divide the dough into six equal parts.
7. Hand-form each bagel into a 4-inch diameter, approximately ¼-inch thick. Place on a cookie sheet and cut the center out (optional), or use a donut pan to form your bagels.
8. Bake them until golden brown or approximately 40 minutes.
9. Take out of the oven and allow to cool slightly or enjoy warm.

Cinnamon Roll Muffins

Total Prep & Cooking Time: 20 min.

Yields: 12 Serving

Nutrition Facts: Calories: 112 | Proteins: 5 g | Carbohydrates: 3g | Fats: 9 g

Ingredients

½ c. of the following:

- coconut oil
- pumpkin puree
- almond butter
- almond flour

1 tbsp. cinnamon

1 t. baking powder

2 scoops vanilla protein powder

For the Icing:

2 t. lemon juice

1 tbsp. sweetener of choice

1/4 c. of the following:

- coconut butter
- milk of choice

Follow these simple steps:

1. Set the oven to 350 setting.
2. Prepare your 12-count muffin pan with muffin liners.
3. Combine protein powder, cinnamon, flour, and baking powder, combining well in a big mixing bowl.
4. Next, add the coconut oil, pumpkin, and butter and mix until fully incorporated.
5. Divide the batter into muffin liners.
6. Slide into the oven, baking for 10 to 15 minutes.
7. After removing from the oven, leave the muffins in tin to cool for five minutes then carefully place on a cooling rack. While cooling, prepare the icing by mixing lemon juice, sweetener, coconut butter, and milk.
8. Drizzle over cooled muffin tops; allow them to sit for 2 to 5 minutes while icing the firms.
9. Serve and enjoy.

Chapter 5: Lunch & Dinner Favorites

It's time to kick up your taste buds with these dishes for lunch or dinner

Mushroom Steak

Total Prep & Cooking Time: 1 hr. 30 min.

Yields: 8 Servings

Nutrition Facts: Calories: 87 | Carbohydrates: 6.2 g | Proteins: 3 g | Fats: 6.2 g

Ingredients:

1 tbsp. of the following:

- fresh lemon juice
- olive oil, extra virgin

2 tbsp. coconut oil

3 thyme sprigs

8 medium Portobello mushrooms

For Sauce:

1 ½ t. of the following:
- minced garlic
- minced peeled fresh ginger

2 tbsp. of the following:
- light brown sugar
- mirin

½ c. low-sodium soy sauce

Follow these simple steps:

1. For the sauce, combine all the sauce ingredients, along with ¼ cup water into a little pan and simmer to cook. Cook using a medium heat until it reduces to a glaze, approximately 15 to 20 minutes, then remove from the heat.
2. For the mushrooms, bring the oven to 350 heat setting.
3. Using a skillet, melt coconut oil and olive oil, cooking the

mushrooms on each side for about 3 minutes.
4. Next, arrange the mushrooms in a single layer on a sheet for baking and season with lemon juice, salt, and pepper.
5. Carefully slide into the oven and roast for 5 minutes. Let it rest for 2 minutes.
6. Plate and drizzle the sauce over the mushrooms.
7. Enjoy.

Spicy Grilled Tofu Steak

Total Prep & Cooking Time: 20 min.

Yields: 4 Servings

Nutrition Facts: Calories: 155 | Carbohydrates: 7.6 g | Proteins: 9.9 g | Fats: 11.8 g

Ingredients:

1 tbsp. of the following:
- chopped scallion
- chopped cilantro
- soy sauce
- hoisin sauce

2 tbsp. oil

¼ t. of the following:
- salt
- garlic powder
- red chili pepper powder
- ground Sichuan peppercorn powder

½ t. cumin

1 pound firm tofu

Follow these simple steps:

1. Place the tofu on a plate and drain the excess liquid for about 10 minutes.

2. Slice drained tofu into ¾ thick stakes.
3. Stir the cumin, Sichuan peppercorn, chili powder, garlic powder, and salt in a mixing bowl until well-incorporated.
4. In another little bowl, combine soy sauce, hoisin, and 1 teaspoon of oil.
5. Heat a skillet to medium temperature with oil, then carefully place the tofu in the skillet.
6. Sprinkle the spices over the tofu, distributing equally across all steaks. Cook for 3-5 minutes, flip, and put spice on the other side. Cook for an additional 3 minutes.
7. Brush with sauce and plate.
8. Sprinkle some scallion and cilantro and enjoy.

Piquillo Salsa Verde Steak

Total Prep & Cooking Time: 25 min.

Yields: 8 Servings

Nutrition Facts: Calories: 427 | Carbohydrates: 67.5 g | Proteins: 14.2 g | Fats: 14.6 g

Ingredients:

4 – ½ inch thick slices of ciabatta

18 oz. firm tofu, drained

5 tbsp. olive oil, extra virgin

Pinch of cayenne

½ t. cumin, ground

1 ½ tbsp. sherry vinegar

1 shallot, diced

8 piquillo peppers (can be from a jar) – drained and cut to ½ inch strips

3 tbsp. of the following:
- parsley, finely chopped
- capers, drained and chopped

Follow these simple steps:

1. Place the tofu on a plate to drain the excess liquid, and then slice into 8 rectangle pieces.
2. You can either prepare your grill or use a grill pan. If using

a grill pan, preheat the grill pan.

3. Mix 3 tablespoons of olive oil, cayenne, cumin, vinegar, shallot, parsley, capers, and piquillo peppers in a medium bowl to make our salsa verde. Season to preference with salt and pepper.
4. Using a paper towel, dry the tofu slices.
5. Brush olive oil on each side, seasoning with salt and pepper lightly.
6. Place the bread on the grill and toast for about 2 minutes using medium-high heat.
7. Next, grill the tofu, cooking each side for about 3 minutes or until the tofu is heated through.
8. Place the toasted bread on the plate then the tofu on top of the bread.
9. Gently spoon out the salsa verde over the tofu and serve.

Butternut Squash Steak

Total Prep & Cooking Time: 50 min.

Yields: 4 Servings

Nutrition Facts: Calories: 300 | Carbohydrates: 46 g | Proteins: 5.3 g | Fats: 10.6 g

Ingredients:

2 tbsp. coconut yogurt

½ t. sweet paprika

1 ¼ c. low-sodium vegetable broth

1 sprig thyme

1 finely chopped garlic clove

1 big thinly sliced shallot

1 tbsp. margarine

2 tbsp. olive oil, extra virgin

Salt and pepper to liking

Follow these simple steps:

1. Bring the oven to 375 heat setting.
2. Cut the squash, lengthwise, into 4 steaks.
3. Carefully core one side of each squash with a paring knife in a crosshatch pattern.
4. Using a brush, coat with olive oil each side of the steak then season generously with salt and pepper.

5. In an oven-safe, non-stick skillet, bring 2 tablespoons of olive oil to a warm temperature.
6. Place the steaks on the skillet with the cored side down and cook at medium temperature until browned, approximately 5 minutes.
7. Flip and repeat on the other side for about 3 minutes.
8. Place the skillet into the oven to roast the squash for 7 minutes.
9. Take out from the oven, placing on a plate and covering with aluminum foil to keep warm.
10. Using the previously used skillet, add thyme, garlic, and shallot, cooking at medium heat. Stir frequently for about 2 minutes.
11. Add brandy and cook for an additional minute.
12. Next, add paprika and whisk the mixture together for 3 minutes.
13. Add in the yogurt seasoning with salt and pepper.
14. Plate the steaks and spoon the sauce over the top.
15. Garnish with parsley and enjoy!

Cauliflower Steak Kicking Corn

Total Prep & Cooking Time: 60 min.

Yields: 6 Servings

Nutrition Facts: Calories: 153 | Carbohydrates: 15 g | Proteins: 4 g | Fats: 10 g

Ingredients:

2 t. capers, drained

4 scallions, chopped

1 red chili, minced

¼ c. vegetable oil

2 ears of corn, shucked

2 big cauliflower heads

Salt and pepper to taste

Follow these simple steps:

1. Heat the oven to 375 degrees.
2. Boil a pot of water, about 4 cups, using the maximum heat setting available.
3. Add corn in the saucepan, cooking approximately 3 minutes or until tender.
4. Drain and allow the corn to cool, then slice the kernels away from the cob.
5. Warm 2 tablespoons of vegetable oil in a skillet.
6. Combine the chili pepper with the oil, cooking for

approximately 30 seconds.
7. Next, combine the scallions, sautéing with the chili pepper until soft.
8. Mix in the corn and capers in the skillet and cook for approximately 1 minute to blend the flavors. Then remove from heat.
9. Warm 1 tablespoon of vegetable oil in a skillet. Once warm, begin to place cauliflower steaks to the pan, 2 to 3 at a time. Season to your liking with salt and cook over medium heat for 3 minutes or until lightly browned.
10. Once cooked, slide onto the cookie sheet and repeat step 5 with the remaining cauliflower.
11. Take the corn mixture and press into the spaces between the florets of the cauliflower.
12. Bake for 25 minutes.
13. Serve warm and enjoy!

Pistachio Watermelon Steak

Total Prep & Cooking Time: 10 min.

Yields: 4 Servings

Nutrition Facts: Calories: 67 | Carbohydrates: 3.8 g | Proteins: 1.6 g | Fats: 5.9 g

Ingredients:

Microgreens

Pistachios chopped

Malden sea salt

1 tbsp. olive oil, extra virgin

1 watermelon

Salt to taste

Follow these simple steps:

1. Begin by cutting the ends of the watermelon.
2. Carefully peel the skin from the watermelon along the white outer edge.
3. Slice the watermelon into 4 slices, approximately 2 inches thick.
4. Trim the slices, so they are rectangular in shape approximately 2 x4 inches.
5. Heat a skillet to medium heat add 1 tablespoon of olive oil.
6. Add watermelon steaks and cook until the edges begin to caramelize.

7. Plate and top with pistachios and microgreens.
8. Sprinkle with Malden salt.
9. Serve warm and enjoy!

BBQ Ribs

Total Prep & Cooking Time: 45 min.

Yields: 2 Servings

Nutrition Facts: Calories: 649 | Carbohydrates: 114 g | Proteins: 34.8 g | Fats: 11.1 g

Ingredients:

2 drops liquid smoke

2 tbsp. of the following:

- soy sauce
- tahini

1 c. of the following:

- water
- wheat gluten

1 tbsp. of the following:
- garlic powder
- onion powder
- lemon pepper

2 t. chipotle powder

For the Sauce:

2 chipotle peppers in adobo, minced

1 tbsp. of the following:
- vegan Worcestershire sauce
- lemon juice
- horseradish
- onion powder
- garlic powder
- ground pepper

1 t. dry mustard

2 tbsp. sweetener of your choice

5 tbsp. brown sugar

½ c. apple cider vinegar

2 c. ketchup

1 c. water

1 freshly squeezed orange juice

Follow these simple steps:

1. Set the oven to 350 heat setting, and prepare the grill charcoal as recommended for this, but gas will work as well.
2. Combine soy sauce, tahini, water, and liquid smoke in a bowl. Then set this mixture to the side in a mixing bowl.
3. Next, use a big glass bowl to mix chipotle powder, onion powder, lemon pepper, garlic powder; combine well then whisk in the ingredients from the little bowl.
4. Add the wheat gluten and mix until it comes to a gooey consistency.
5. Grease a standard-size loaf pan and transfer the mixture to the loaf pan. Smooth it out so that the rib mixture fits flat in the pan.
6. Bake for 30 minutes.
7. While the mixture is baking, make the BBQ sauce. To make the sauce, combine all the sauce ingredients in a pot. Allow the mixture to simmer its way to the boiling point to combine the flavors, and as soon as it boils, decrease the heat to the minimum setting. Let it be for 10 more minutes.
8. Cautiously take the rib out of the oven and slide onto a plate.
9. Coat the top rib mixture with the BBQ Sauce and place on the grill.

10. Coat the other side of the rib mixture with BBQ Sauce and grill for 6 minutes
11. Flip and grill the other side for an additional 6 minutes.
12. Serve warm and enjoy!

Spicy Veggie Steaks With veggies

Total Prep & Cooking Time: 45 mins.

Yields: 4 Servings

Nutrition Facts: Calories: 458 | Carbohydrates: 65.5 g | Proteins: 39.1 g | Fats: 7.6 g

Ingredients:

1 ¾ c. vital wheat gluten

½ c. vegetable stock

¼ t. liquid smoke

1 tbsp. Dijon mustard

1 t. paprika

½ c. tomato paste

2 tbsp. soy sauce

½ t. oregano

¼ t. of the following:
- coriander powder
- cumin

1 t. of the following:
- onion powder
- garlic powder

¼ c. nutritional yeast

¾ c. canned chickpeas

Marinade:

½ t. red pepper flakes

2 cloves garlic, minced

2 tbsp. soy sauce

1 tbsp. lemon juice, freshly squeezed

¼ c. maple syrup

For skewers:

15 skewers, soaked in water for 30 minutes if wooden

¾ t. salt

8 oz. zucchini or yellow summer squash

¼ t. ground black pepper

1 tbsp. olive oil

1 red onion, medium

Follow these simple steps:

1. In a food processor, add chickpeas, vegetable stock, liquid smoke, Dijon mustard, pepper, paprika, tomato paste, soy sauce, oregano, coriander, cumin, onion powder, garlic, and natural yeast. Process until the ingredients are well-mixed.
2. Add the vital wheat gluten to a big mixing bowl, and pour the contents from the food processor into the center. Mix with a spoon until a soft dough is formed.
3. Knead the dough for approximately 2 minutes; do not over knead.

4. Once the dough is firm and stretchy, flatten it to create 4 equal-sized steaks.
5. Individually wrap the steaks in tin foil; be sure not to wrap the steaks too tightly, as they will expand when steaming.
6. Steam for 20 minutes. To steam, you can use any steamer you like or a basket over boiling water.
7. While steaming, prepare the marinade. In a bowl, whisk the red pepper, garlic, soy sauce, lemon juice, and syrup. Reserve half of the sauce for brushing during grilling.
8. Prepare the skewers. Cut the onion and zucchini or yellow squash into 1/2-inch chunks.
9. In a glass bowl, add the red onion, zucchini, and yellow squash then coat with olive oil, pepper, and salt to taste. Place the vegetables on the skewers.
10. After the steaks have steamed for 20 minutes, unwrap and place on a cookie sheet. Pour the marinade over the steaks, fully covering them.
11. Bring your skewers, steaks, and glaze to the grill. Place the skewers on the grill over direct heat. Brush skewers with glaze. Grill for approximately 3 minutes then flip.
12. Place the steaks directly on the grill, glaze side down, and brush the top with additional glaze. Cook to your desired doneness.
13. Serve warm and enjoy!

Tofu Seitan

Total Prep & Cooking Time: 1 hr, 40 mins.

Yields: 6 Servings

Nutrition Facts: Calories: 159 | Carbohydrates: 8 g | Proteins: 26 g | Fats: 2 g

Ingredients:

½ t. salt

1 t. garlic, powdered

2 t. vegetable broth

1 tbsp. onion, powdered

2 tbsp. of the following

- nutritional yeast
- water

1 ¼ c. tofu

1 ½ c. vital wheat gluten

Follow these simple steps:

1. Stir together the ingredients above in a bowl until a dough forms.
2. Lightly dust the countertop and your hands with wheat gluten. Using the counter service, form a ball out of the dough. Be careful not to knead it because it might make the seitan tough.

3. Once the ball is formed, cut it into 6 equal pieces.
4. Using your fingers press each ball into an oval shape, about 4x6 inches.
5. With a steamer basket placed inside a big pot, add water into the bottom of the pot and bring it to a rolling boil.
6. Place the seitan into the steamer basket; if they overlap, brush them with oil to prevent them from sticking.
7. Cover and steam for approximately 12 minutes then flip so that both sides steam evenly.
8. Once steamed on both sides, remove and allow cooling for a minimum of 1 hour.
9. The tenders are fully cooked at this point, so you can reheat them or toss them on the grill with your favorite sauce, or you can eat them cold over leafy greens.
10. Enjoy!

Stuffed Zucchini

Total Prep & Cooking Time: 30 mins.

Yields: 4 Servings

Nutrition Facts: Calories: 159 | Carbohydrates: 8 g | Proteins: 26 g | Fats: 2 g

Ingredients:

1 ½ c. black beans, drained

¼ t. chili powder

½ of the following:

- sea salt
- cumin, ground

1 of the following

- clove garlic, minced
- red bell pepper, diced
- red onion, diced

1 tbsp. olive oil, extra virgin

4 medium zucchini

For the Sauce

¼ t. of the following:

- chili powder
- turmeric
- sea salt

1 tbsp. Nutritional yeast

½ t. apple cider vinegar

¼ c. of the following:

- water
- raw tahini

4 t. Lemon juice

Follow these simple steps:

1. Set the oven to 350 heat setting.
2. Slice the knobs off the top and bottom of the zucchini, and then slice in half lengthwise.
3. Scoop the center of the seeds from each zucchini with a spoon, creating a bowl to hold the filling.
4. On a big cookie sheet, place the zucchini bowls and bake for approximately 20 minutes.
5. Using a big skillet, combine onion and pepper and sauté for five minutes at medium-high temperature until softened.
6. Add garlic and sauté for an additional minute.
7. Turn the skillet down to medium heat and sprinkle in the chili powder, cumin, salt, and black beans and warm. Remove from the stove and cover to maintain warmth.
8. Prepare the sauce. Using a little bowl, whisk the sauce ingredients until smooth and creamy.
9. Remove the zucchini from the oven when finished cooking.

10. Fill each zucchini bowl generously with the bean mixture.

11. Drizzle the sauce over.

12. Serve warm and enjoy!

Roasted Butternut Squash With Chimichurri

Total Prep & Cooking Time: 30 mins.

Yields: 2 Servings

Nutrition Facts: Calories: 615 | Carbohydrates: 71.6 g | Proteins: 12.5 g | Fats: 35.7 g

Ingredients:

1 c. onion, thinly sliced

2 cloves garlic

1 tbsp. coconut oil

1 acorn squash

2 tbsp. olive oil (best if extra virgin)

¼ c. goji berries

1 c. water

2 c. mushrooms, sliced

½ c. quinoa

Chimichurri Sauce

½ t. salt

2 tbsp. lime

½ c. olive oil, extra virgin

¼ t. cayenne pepper

1 shallot

3 cloves garlic

1 tbsp. sherry vinegar

1 c. parsley

Follow these simple steps:

1. Bring the broiler to the maximum heat setting.
2. Stir up the chimichurri sauce by combining the parsley, vinegar, garlic shallot, cayenne pepper, olive oil, lime juice, and ½ cup of olive oil. Blend well; if you want the sauce a little thinner, then add additional extra virgin oil.
3. Prepare an aluminum-foiled cookie sheet.
4. Divide the squash in half by carefully cutting widthwise, and remove seeds and pulp from the center.
5. Cut each half of the squash into moon shape slices; you should get about 4-6 slices.
6. Place the slices on the aluminum foil sheet and spritz olive oil across the top.
7. Keep a close eye on the squash; you want nice char marks, nothing more. Once one side is charred to your liking, flip the squash and char the other side.
8. While broiling, bring a medium-sized saucepan of water to a rolling boil then simmer the quinoa, cooking for 10 minutes or until tender.

9. Heat a skillet to medium heat, and sauté the onions. Once the onions are caramelizing, add in the mushroom and garlic, cooking on low heat for approximately 5 minutes.
10. Plate the squash, topping it with quinoa and mushroom.
11. Sprinkle goji berries across the plate and drizzle chimichurri sauce.
12. Serve warm and enjoy!

Eggplant Pizza

Total Prep & Cooking Time: 30 mins.

Yields: 8 Servings

Nutrition Facts: Calories: 234 | Carbohydrates: 27 g | Proteins: 5.4 g | Fats: 12 g

Ingredients:

2 tbsp. olive oil

¼ t. of the following:

- pepper
- salt

½ t. oregano, dried

1 c. panko

½ tbsp. almond flour

1 tbsp. flaxseed, ground

1/3 c. water

½ eggplant, medium size

2 c. marinara sauce

1 lb. vegan pizza dough

For the cheese:

¼ lb. tofu, extra firm drained

2 tbsp. almond milk, unsweetened

½ c. cashews, soaked for 6 hours, drained

3 tbsp. lemon juice, freshly squeezed

Follow these simple steps:

1. Set the oven to 400 heat setting; prepare a cookie sheet with ½ tablespoon of olive oil by brushing to coat.
2. Whisk together flaxseed, flour, and water in a little bowl.
3. In a different bowl, combine salt, pepper, oregano, and panko.
4. Prepare the eggplant by slicing into ¼ inch triangles.
5. Dip each eggplant triangle into the flaxseed mixture then coat with panko mixture and place on the cookie sheet.
6. Slide gently into the oven and baking for 15 minutes. Flip and then bake for an additional 15 minutes or until lightly browned.
7. Take out of the oven and set to the side.
8. Get a pizza stone or pizza pan ready for the dough.
9. Lightly flour the workspace, and with a rolling pin, work the dough to a 14-inch circle then transfer to the pizza stone or pizza pan.
10. Brush the dough's top with olive oil and slide into the warm oven, cooking until lightly browned or for about twenty minutes.
11. While the crust is baking, prepare the cheese by placing cashews in the high-speed blender, blending until it reaches a crumbly consistency.
12. Then add to the blender the lemon juice, almond milk, and

tofu; blend until it's a chunky cheese-like consistency. Set to the side.
13. Once the crust is cooked, assemble the pizza by saucing crust with marinara, adding eggplant slices, and placing the cheese on top.
14. Serve warm and enjoy!

Green Avocado Carbonara

Total Prep & Cooking Time: 15 mins.
Yields: 1 Servings
Nutrition Facts: Calories: 526 | Carbohydrates: 24.6 g | Proteins: 5.8 g | Fats: 48.7 g

Ingredients:

Spinach angel hair
Parsley, fresh
2 t. olive oil, extra virgin
2 cloves garlic, diced
½ lemon, zest, and juice
1 avocado, pitted
Salt and pepper to taste

Follow these simple steps:

1. Combine using a food processor the parsley, olive oil,

garlic, lemon, and avocado and blend until smooth.
2. Prepare the noodles according to package.
3. Place noodles in a bowl, and add the sauce on top of noodles.
4. Add pepper and salt to your liking.
5. Serve warm and enjoy!

Curried Tofu

Total Prep & Cooking Time: 30 mins.

Yields: 4 Servings

Nutrition Facts: Calories: 345 | Carbohydrates: 37 g | Proteins: 33.9 g | Fats: 6.3 g

Ingredients:

¼ t. garlic powder

2 tbsp. curry powder

1 pack extra firm tofu

Follow these simple steps:

1. Heat to 400 degrees the oven.
2. Slice the tofu into cubes.
3. In a container with a lid, add the garlic powder, curry powder, and cubed tofu.
4. Close it tightly and shake lightly just to coat the tofu. Make

sure there's even coverage of the spices.
5. On a parchment-lined cookie sheet, place the tofu cubes and bake for 15 minutes, flip and continue baking for another 15 minutes or until crisp.
6. Serve warm and enjoy!

Sesame Tofu and Eggplant

Total Prep & Cooking Time: 20 mins.

Yields: 4 Servings

Nutrition Facts: Calories: 295 | Carbohydrates: 6.87 g | Proteins: 11.21 g | Fats: 6.87 g

Ingredients:

1 tbsp. olive oil

¼ c. of the following:

- sesame seeds
- soy sauce

1 eggplant

1 pound firm tofu

1 t. crushed red pepper flakes

2 cloves garlic

2 t. sweetener of your choice

4 tbsp. toasted sesame oil

1 c. cilantro, chopped

3 tbsp. rice vinegar

Salt and pepper to taste

Follow these simple steps:

1. Set the oven to 200 heat setting.
2. Remove the tofu from the package and blot using paper

towels to absorb excess moisture.
3. In a big mixing bowl, whisk together red pepper flakes, garlic, sesame oil, vinegar, and ¼ cup of cilantro to create the marinade.
4. With a mandolin, julienne the eggplant. If you do not have this, you can create the noodles by hand.
5. Mix the noodles in the big bowl with the marinade.
6. Add oil to a skillet over medium-low flame setting, and cook the eggplant until soft.
7. Turn off the oven, and add the last of the cilantro.
8. Transfer the contents from the skillet to an oven-safe dish, cover with foil, and place in the oven to keep warm.
9. Cut the tofu into 8 slices and coat with sesame seeds. Press the sesame seeds into the tofu.
10. In the skillet, add 2 tablespoons of sesame oil and warm under medium heat. Fry the tofu for five minutes then flip and fry.
11. Pour the soy sauce into the pan, coating the tofu. Cook until the tofu looks caramelized.
12. Remove the noodles from the oven and plate with the tofu on top of the noodles.
13. Serve warm and enjoy!

Tempeh Coconut Curry

Total Prep & Cooking Time: 30 mins.

Yields: 4 Servings

Nutrition Facts: Calories: 558 | Carbohydrates: 54.2 g | Proteins: 18.4 g | Fats: 33.5 g

Curry:

2 t. of the following:

- low-sodium soy sauce
- tamarind pulp

1 tbsp. of the following:

- lime juice
- garlic, finely chopped
- ginger, finely chopped
- vegetable oil
- salt

8 oz. tempeh

13.5 oz. coconut milk, light

1 c. water

3 c. sweet potato, chopped

1 cinnamon stick

½ t. of the following:
- red pepper, crushed
- turmeric, ground

1 ½ t. coriander, ground

2 c. onion, finely chopped

Rice:

1 ½ c. cauliflower rice

¼ t. salt

1/3 c. cilantro, chopped

Follow these simple steps:

1. Using a medium-high heat setting, warm some oil in a big pot or whatever you prefer, as long as it's nonstick.
2. Place the onion and ½ teaspoon of salt and sauté for approximately 2 minutes.
3. Next, stir in the tamarind, breaking it up as you combine in the skillet and cooking for another 2 minutes.
4. Add in the ginger, garlic, coriander, turmeric, crushed red pepper, and cinnamon stick; stir constantly.
5. Add in the additional salt, tempeh, milk, water, and

potatoes, bringing to a boil.
6. Cover, allowing to simmer for fifteen minutes or until tender.
7. Whisk in the soy sauce and simmer for 3 additional minutes.
8. Remove the cinnamon stick.
9. Cook the cauliflower rice according to package instructions.
10. Stir in the cilantro.
11. Place the rice in a bowl and cover with curry.
12. Serve warm and enjoy!

Tempeh Tikka Masala

Total Prep & Cooking Time: 1 h, 35 mins.

Yields: 3 Servings

Nutrition Facts: Calories: 430 | Carbohydrates: 39 g | Proteins: 21 g | Fats: 23 g

Tempeh:

½ t. sea salt

1 t. of the following:

- gram masala
- ginger, ground
- cumin, ground

2 t. apple cider vinegar

½ c. vegan yogurt

8 oz. tempeh, cubed

Tikka Masala Sauce:

2 c. frozen peas

1 c. of the following:

- full-fat coconut milk
- tomato sauce

¼ t. turmeric

½ t. sea salt

1 onion, chopped

1 t. of the following:

- chili powder
- garam masala

1/4 c. ginger, freshly grated
3 cloves garlic, minced
1 tbsp. coconut oil

Follow these simple steps:

1. Begin with making the tempeh by combining sea salt, garam masala, ginger, cumin, vinegar, and yogurt in a bowl.
2. Add tempeh to the bowl and coat well; cover the bowl and refrigerate for 60 minutes.
3. In a pan big enough for 3 servings, add some coconut oil to heat using the medium setting, and begin preparing the sauce.
4. Sauté in the ginger, garlic, and onion for 5 minutes or until fragrant.
5. Add the garam masala, chili powder, sea salt, and turmeric and combine well.
6. Add the frozen peas, coconut, milk, tomato sauce, and tempeh, reducing the heat to medium.
7. Simmer for 15 minutes
8. Remove from the heat and serve with cauliflower rice.

Caprice Casserole

Total Prep & Cooking Time: 1 h, 35 mins.

Yields: 3 Servings

Nutrition Facts: Calories: 642 | Carbohydrates: 88.6 g | Proteins: 25.1 g | Fats: 5.1 g

Tempeh:

¼ c. basil, chopped

1 tomato, big

¼ t. pepper

½ t. salt

1 tbsp. of the following:

- nutritional yeast
- tahini

1 clove garlic

14 oz. tofu, extra firm, drained

6 cups marinara sauce

10 oz. vegetable noodles

Follow these simple steps:

1. Set the oven to 350 heat setting.
2. Cut the tofu into 4 slabs and remove excess moisture by gently squeezing each slab with a paper towel.
3. In a food processor, add garlic and chop, then scrape

garlic from the sides to ensure it will be thoroughly mixed.
4. Add pepper, salt, yeast, tahini, and tofu to the food processor and pulse for 15 to 20 seconds until fully combined and forming a paste.
5. In an oven-safe dish, spread ½ cup of the marinara sauce across the bottom.
6. Divide the vegetable noodles in half, break the noodles, and layer them on top of the sauce.
7. Add another layer of sauce on top of the noodles.
8. Add the remaining noodles and coat the top with remaining sauce.
9. Using the tofu mixture from the food processor, form little patties about ½ thick and place on top of the sauce, filling up the dish.
10. Cover the baking container with aluminum foil and bake for 20 minutes.
11. Uncover and bake for an additional fifteen minutes.
12. Remove from the oven and set the oven to broil.
13. Place the tomato slices on top of tofu mixture and broil for 2 minutes or until the tofu is lightly toasted.
14. Garnish with basil.
15. Serve warm and enjoy.

Cheesy Brussel Sprout Bake

Total Prep & Cooking Time: 45 mins.

Yields: 8 Servings

Nutrition Facts: Calories: 116 | Carbohydrates: 16 g | Proteins: 4 g | Fats: 4 g

Ingredients:

½ onion sliced

2 tbsp. of each of these

- garlic, chopped
- avocado oil

1 ½ lb. Brussel sprouts

Cheese:

Dash cayenne

1 t. of the following:

- onion powder
- salt

¼ t. of the following:

- pepper
- paprika

½ t. of the following:

- garlic, powder
- thyme

1 tbsp. tapioca starch

¼ c. nutritional yeast

½ c. vegetable broth

1 can coconut cream

Crumble Topping :

¼ t. pepper

½ t. garlic, powder

1 t. salt

½ c. panko crumbs

Follow these simple steps:

1. Bring the oven to 425 heat setting.
2. Prepare Brussel sprouts by washing and trimming then steaming for 10 minutes.
3. Spray an oven-safe baking dish with nonstick spray.
4. Add the Brussel sprouts to a baking dish and set to the side.
5. Bring a skillet to medium temperature and mix in the garlic, avocado oil, and onion, sautéing approximately 6 minutes.
6. Add the onion mixture to the top of the Brussel sprouts.
7. In the same skillet on low heat, add vegetable broth, nutritional yeast, onion powder, pepper, salt, garlic, paprika, thyme, and coconut cream, whisking together to combine.

8. Carefully add in the tapioca starch and whisk constantly; the mixture will thicken in about 5 minutes. Once it turns into a cheese sauce mixture, pour over the Brussel sprouts and onions.
9. In a mixing container, combine panko, salt, garlic, and pepper, creating the crumble.
10. Sprinkle the crumble across the top of the cheese.
11. Cook in the oven for approximately 25 minutes or until browned and golden.
12. Serve warm and enjoy.

Tofu Noodle Bowl

Total Prep & Cooking Time: 45 mins.

Yields: 4 Servings

Nutrition Facts: Calories: 669 | Carbohydrates: 69 g | Proteins: 55.1 g | Fats: 24.7g

Ingredients:

¼ c. of the following
- peanuts, chopped
- cilantro, chopped

4 heads baby bok choy, chopped

2 packages premade baked tofu, 8 oz.

½ t. black pepper, ground

2 t. of the following:
- turmeric, ground
- garlic chili sauce

1 tbsp. of the following:
- lime juice
- ginger, minced

2 c. vegetable stock

2 carrots, julienned

1 red bell pepper, chopped

½ red onion, diced

2 cloves garlic, minced

1 t. peanut oil

6 oz. Thai rice noodles

Follow these simple steps:

1. Prepare the Thai noodles, following the package guidelines or according to your preference.
2. Warm a big pan using medium-high heat, adding in the peanut oil.
3. Sauté the ginger, garlic, and onion for approximately 5 minutes.
4. Next, add in the carrots and bell pepper, stirring frequently and cooking for 5 minutes.
5. Whisk together the lime juice, black pepper, turmeric, chili sauce, and stock, then combine with the pan of peppers and carrots.
6. Wait for the mixture to boil, and soon after, bring down the heat setting, and leave it cooking for nearly 5 minutes.
7. As it simmers, add in the noodles, bok choy, and tofu and cook for an additional 5 minutes.
8. Divide between bowls and garnish with chili peppers, peanuts, and cilantro.
9. Serve warm and enjoy.

Cashew Siam Salad

Total Prep & Cooking Time: 25 mins.

Yields: 4 Servings

Nutrition Facts: Calories: 352 | Carbohydrates: 26.6 g | Proteins: 9.6 g | Fats: 24.5 g

Ingredients:

3 green onions, chopped

2/3 c. sunflower seeds

1 bag slaw mix

2 packages ramen noodles

1 c. cashews, crushed

1 t. olive oil

Dressing:

Seasoning packets from ramen noodles

1 c. vinegar

½ c. sweetener of your choice

Follow these simple steps:

1. Set the oven to 350 heat setting.
2. In a mixing container, combine cashews and oil and mix until the nuts are lightly oiled.
3. Place the nuts on a lined cookie sheet and toast until lightly browned in the oven.
4. In a big mixing bowl, crumble the ramen noodles and combine with slaw mix, sunflower seeds, and green onion.
5. Whisk together the vinegar and sweetener of your choice in a little bowl until combined.
6. Remove the peanuts from the oven and cool.
7. Place the salad in a bowl and cover the top with peanuts.
8. When ready to serve, add the dressing, and enjoy.

Cucumber Edamame Salad

Total Prep & Cooking Time: 2 hours mins.

Yields: 8 Servings

Nutrition Facts: Calories: 166 | Carbohydrates: 6.4 g | Proteins: 2.9 g | Fats: 14.9 g

Ingredients:

1 jalapeno pepper, seeded and chopped

2 c. froze edamame, shelled and thawed

4 English cucumbers, spiralizer

Vinaigrette:

1 t. red pepper flakes

1 ½ t. of the following:

- garlic
- Dijon mustard
- soy sauce, low-sodium

2 t. ginger, paste

3 t. toasted sesame oil

1/3 c. of the following:

- rice vinegar
- extra virgin olive oil

Follow these simple steps:

1. Begin by cleaning your cucumbers and spiraling them to create the noodles.
2. Once cucumbers are spiraled, use a towel or cheesecloth to discard the excess moisture out of the noodles.
3. In a big mixing bowl, add noodles, jalapeno, red bell pepper, and edamame. Carefully toss the salad mixture and set to the side.
4. In a little mixing container, prepare the vinaigrette by whisking together the red pepper flakes, garlic, Dejon, soy sauce, ginger, oil, rice vinegar, and olive oil.
5. Lightly coat the salad with dressing.
6. Cover and refrigerate overnight or a minimum of 2 hours.
7. Serve cool and enjoy.

Caesar Vegan Salad

Total Prep & Cooking Time: 30 mins.

Yields: 6 Servings

Nutrition Facts: Calories: 284 | Carbohydrates: 25.5 g | Proteins: 8.7 g | Fats: 18.4 g

Ingredients:

5 c. kale, chopped

10 c. romaine lettuce

Cheese:

½ t. garlic

1 tbsp. of the following:

- extra virgin olive oil
- nutritional yeast

1 garlic clove

2 tbsp. hemp seeds, hulled

1/3 c. cashews, raw

Caesar Dressing:

½ t. of the following:

- sea salt
- garlic powder
- Dijon mustard

2 t. capers

½ tbsp. vegan Worcestershire sauce

2 tbsp. olive oil (best if extra virgin)

½ c. raw cashews, soaked overnight

¼ c. water

1 clove garlic, crushed

1 tbsp. lemon juice

Croutons:

1/8 t. cayenne pepper

½ t. of the following:
- garlic powder
- sea salt

1 t. olive oil, (best if extra virgin)

14 oz. can chickpeas

Follow these simple steps:

1. On the day before you plan to make this salad, in a little bowl, soak ½ c. of the raw cashews overnight then drain and rinse.
2. For the Croutons – Bring the oven to 400 heat setting. Drain the chickpeas and rinse thoroughly. Using a tea towel or cheesecloth, rub the chickpeas so that the skins fall off. Place those in a dish for baking. Spritz the chickpeas with oil and roll them around to coat. Season with cayenne, salt, and garlic powder. Roast the chickpeas

for approximately a quarter of an hour or until you are satisfied with the color. Remove from the oven, allowing to cool and become firm.

3. For the Dressing – Combine everything but not the salt, either in a processor or blender. Blend until smooth liquid consistency. If needed, add ½ tablespoon of water at a time until you have a dressing-like consistency. Season with salt to taste. Set to the side.
4. For the Cheese – In a food processor, add garlic and cashews and process them until they reach a finely chopped consistency. Add hemp seeds, nutritional yeast, olive oil, and garlic powder and blend until combined. Season with salt to taste.
5. For the lettuce – After washing the kale, finely chop and set to the side. Chop the lettuce roughly into 2-inch pieces and toss with the kale in a bowl.
6. Pour some dressing and toss again to coat the greens fully.
7. Sprinkle the cheese and croutons over the top.
8. Serve cool and enjoy.

Mushroom Lettuce Wraps

Total Prep & Cooking Time: 30 mins.

Yields: 4 Servings

Nutrition Facts: Calories: 265 | Carbohydrates: 37.6 g | Proteins: 13.6 g | Fats: 7.9 g

Ingredients:

8 big leaf romaine lettuce

4 green onions, sliced

¼ t. red pepper flakes

2 t. of the following:

- ginger, grated
- canola oil

2 cloves garlic

12 oz. extra firm tofu

1 t. sesame oil

2 tbsp. rice vinegar

8 oz. mushrooms, diced

1 can water chestnuts

3 tbsp. of the following:

- soy sauce, reduced-sodium
- hoisin Sauce

Follow these simple steps:

1. Whisk together in a little bowl the sesame oil, rice vinegar, soy sauce, and hoisin. Then set to the side.
2. Open the tofu, and using a paper towel or cheesecloth, remove as much liquid as you can.
3. In a big skillet over medium-high heat, warm the 2 teaspoons of canola oil.
4. Crumble the tofu, making it into little pieces and cook for approximately 5 minutes.
5. Add in the diced mushrooms and cook until almost all the liquid evaporates.
6. Add in the green onions, red pepper, ginger, garlic, and chestnuts and cook for about 30 seconds.
7. Pour the sauce from the little bowl into the skillet and cook until sauce is thoroughly warmed.
8. Plate the individual lettuce leaves and spoon the tofu mixture into each lettuce wrap.
9. Serve and enjoy warm.

Chapter 6: Side Dishes & Snacks

For those special occasions, just prepare a tasty snack or a beautiful side dish.

Mixed Seed Crackers

Total Prep & Cooking Time: 60 min.

Yields: 30 Servings

Nutrition Facts: Calories: 61 | Carbohydrates: 1 g | Proteins: 2 g | Fats: 6 g

Ingredients:

1 c. boiling water

¼ c. coconut oil, melted

1 t. salt

1 tbsp. psyllium husk powder

1/3 c. of the following:
- sesame seeds
- flaxseed
- pumpkin seeds, unsalted
- sunflower seeds, unsalted
- almond flour

Follow these simple steps:

1. Set the oven to 300 setting.
2. With a fork, combine the almond flour, seeds, psyllium, and salt.
3. Cautiously pour the boiling water and oil to the bowl, using the fork to combine.
4. The mixture should form a gel-like consistency.
5. Line a cookie sheet using a non-stick paper or a similar alternative, and transfer the mixture to the cookie sheet.
6. Using the second sheet of parchment, place it on top of the mixture, and with a rolling pin, roll out the mixture to an even and flat consistency.
7. Remove the top parchment paper and bake in the oven for 40 minutes, checking frequently to ensure the seeds do not burn.

8. After 40 minutes, or when the seeds are browning, turn off the oven but leave the crackers inside for further cooking.
9. Once cool break into pieces and enjoy

Crispy Squash Chips

Total Prep & Cooking Time: 30 min.

Yields: 2 Servings

Nutrition Facts: Calories: 83 | Carbohydrates: 5.8 g | Proteins: 0.5 g | Fats: 7 g

Ingredients:

1 t. cayenne pepper

1 t. cumin

1 t. paprika

1 tbsp. avocado oil

1 medium butternut squash, skinny neck

Sea salt to taste

Follow these simple steps:

1. Set the oven to 375 heat setting.
2. Prepare the butternut squash by removing the top.
3. Using a mandolin, cut the squash into even slices; it is not necessary to skin the squash.

4. In a big mixing bowl, place your slices of squash and cover with oil, using your hands to mix them well. Ensure all slices are oiled.
5. Line a cookie sheet with parchment paper and spread out your slices, so they do not overlap.
6. In a little bowl, mix together cayenne pepper, paprika, and cumin then sprinkle the chips over the top.
7. Season with sea salt to taste
8. Once cool, enjoy alone or with your favorite dip.

Paprika Nuts

Total Prep & Cooking Time: 30 min.

Yields: 8 Servings

Nutrition Facts: Calories: 417 | Carbohydrates: 12.4 g | Proteins: 10.8 g | Fats: 39.2 g

Ingredients:

1 ½ t. smoked paprika

1 t. salt

2 tbsp. garlic-infused olive oil

1 c. of the following:
- cashews
- almonds
- pecans
- walnuts

Follow these simple steps:

1. Adjust the racks in the oven so that there is one rack in the middle.
2. Set the oven to 325 before you start preparing the ingredients.
3. In a big mixing bowl, toss the nuts.
4. Pour olive oil over the nuts and toss to coat all the nuts.

5. Sprinkle the salt and paprika over the nuts and mix well. If you want more paprika flavor, then add additional paprika.
6. Line a big cookie sheet with parchment and spread the nuts out in one layer.
7. Bake for approximately 15 minutes, then remove from oven and let cool.
8. Enjoy.

Basil Zoodles and Olives

Total Prep & Cooking Time: 4 hr. 30 min.

Yields: 6 Servings

Nutrition Facts: Calories: 117 | Carbohydrates: 9.8 g | Proteins: 3.5 g | Fats: 8.4 g

Ingredients:

1 can black olives pitted

1 little container cherry tomatoes, halved

4 medium-size zucchini

Sauce:

½ c basil leaves, chopped

½ t. pink Himalayan salt

2 t. nutritional yeast

1 tbsp. lemon juice

½ c. water

¼ c. of the following:
- sunflower seeds, soaked
- cashew nuts, soaked

Follow these simple steps:

1. Begin by preparing the sunflower seeds and cashews. Place each in a little bowl and cover with water. Allow to soak for 4 hours then drain and rinse well.
2. Next, place the seeds and cashews into a blender and mix until completely blended. Then add in basil, salt, nutritional yeast, lemon juice, and water. Blend until a smooth sauce is formed.
3. Using a spiralizer, make the zoodles from the zucchini.
4. Place the zoodles in a big serving bowl and then pour the sauce over the top. Stir to combine.
5. Top with cherry tomatoes and olives.
6. Serve and enjoy.

Roasted Beetroot Noodles

Total Prep & Cooking Time: 35 min.

Yields: 4 Servings

Nutrition Facts: Calories: 79 | Carbohydrates: 4.1 g | Proteins: 1 g | Fats: 7 g

Ingredients:

1 t. orange zest

2 tbsp. of the following:
- parsley, chopped
- balsamic vinegar
- olive oil

2 big beets, peeled and spiraled

Follow these simple steps:

1. Set the oven to 425 high-heat setting.
2. In a big bowl, combine the beet noodles, olive oil, and vinegar. Toss until well-combined. Season with salt and pepper to your liking.
3. Line a big cookie sheet with parchment paper, and spread the noodles out into a single layer. Roast the noodles for 20 minutes.
4. Place into bowls and zest with orange and sprinkle parsley. Gently toss and serve.

Turnip Fries

Total Prep & Cooking Time: 45 min.

Yields: 4 Servings

Nutrition Facts: Calories: 83 | Carbohydrates: 11.6 g | Proteins: 3.2 g | Fats: 3.1 g

Ingredients:

1 t. of the following:
- onion powder
- paprika
- garlic salt

1 tbsp. vegetable oil

3 pounds turnips

Follow these simple steps:

1. Set the oven to 425 heat setting.

2. Prepare a lightly greased aluminum foil-lined cookie sheet
3. Using a hand peeler, peel the turnips. With a Mandolin, cut the turnips into French fry sticks. Then place in a big bowl.
4. Toss the turnips with oil to coat then season with onion powder, paprika, and garlic and coat again.
5. Spread evenly across the cookie sheet.
6. Bake for 20 minutes or until the outside is crisp.
7. Serve with your favorite sauce or enjoy alone.

Lime and Chili Carrots Noodles

Total Prep & Cooking Time: 10 min.

Yields: 4 Servings

Nutrition Facts: Calories: 89 | Carbohydrates: 7 g | Proteins: 1 g | Fats: 7 g

Ingredients:

½ t. of the following:
- black pepper
- salt

2 tbsp. coconut oil

¼ c. coriander, finely chopped

2 Jalapeno chili's

1 tbsp. lime juice

2 carrots, peeled and spiralized

Follow these simple steps:

1. In a little bowl, combine jalapeno, lime juice, and coconut oil to form a sauce.
2. In a big bowl, place the carrot noodles and pour dressing over the top.
3. Toss to ensure the dressing fully coats the noodles.
4. Season with salt and pepper to your liking.
5. Serve and enjoy.

Pesto Zucchini Noodles

Total Prep & Cooking Time: 15 min.

Yields: Servings

Nutrition Facts: Calories: 166 | Carbohydrates: 4.5g | Proteins: 1.6 g | Fats: 17 g

Ingredients:

4 little zucchini ends trimmed

Cherry tomatoes

2 t. fresh lemon juice

1/3 c olive oil (best if extra-virgin)

2 cups packed basil leaves

2 c. garlic

Salt and pepper to taste

Follow these simple steps:

1. Spiral zucchini into noodles and set to the side.
2. In a food processor, combine the basil and garlic and chop. Slowly add olive oil while chopping. Then pulse blend it until thoroughly mixed.
3. In a big bowl, place the noodles and pour pesto sauce over the top. Toss to combine.
4. Garnish with tomatoes and serve and enjoy.

Cabbage Slaw

Total Prep & Cooking Time: 5 min.

Yields: 6 Servings

Nutrition Facts: Calories: 276 | Carbohydrates: 11.7 g | Proteins: 0 g | Fats: 9.3 g

Ingredients:

1/8 t. celery seed

¼ t. salt

2 tbsp. of the following:
- apple cider vinegar
- sweetener of your choice

½ c. vegan mayo

4 c. coleslaw mix with red cabbage and carrots

Follow these simple steps:

1. In a big mixing bowl, whisk together the celery seed, salt, apple cider vinegar, sweetener, and vegan mayo.
2. Add the coleslaw and stir until appropriately combined.
3. Refrigerate while covered for a minimum of 2 hours or overnight if you're not in a hurry.
4. Garnish with tomatoes and serve and enjoy.

Zucchini Chips

Total Prep & Cooking Time: 1 hr. 40 min

Yields: 4 Servings

Nutrition Facts: Calories: 276 | Carbohydrates: 11.7 g | Proteins: 0 g | Fats: 9.3 g

Ingredients:

2 tbsp. olive oil (best if extra virgin)

1 big zucchini

½ t. of the following:
- black pepper, ground
- salt

Follow these simple steps:

1. Bring the oven to 400 heat setting.
2. Using a mandolin, slice the zucchini into 1/8th-inch slices.
3. Once sliced, use a paper towel to remove the excess moisture from the zucchini by blotting the tops.
4. Prepare two cookie sheets with parchment paper, and spread the zucchini out into a single layer.
5. Whisk well the olive oil and seasonings. With this mixture, brush each zucchini.
6. Bake this for 60 minutes then flip.

7. Check every 20 minutes, and once the zucchini is crispy, remove from the oven and serve.

Peanut Tofu Wrap

Total Prep & Cooking Time: 30 min

Yields: 4 Servings

Nutrition Facts: Calories: 186 | Carbohydrates: 8 g | Proteins: 13 g | Fats: 12 g

Ingredients:

¼ c. cilantro, finely chopped

1 c. of the following:
- Asian pear
- English cucumber

1 ½ t. lime zest

1 tbsp. of the following:
- rice vinegar
- canola oil

5 tbsp. peanut sauce

14 oz. tofu, extra firm

8 cabbage leaves

Follow these simple steps:

1. Prepare cabbage leaves by washing and drying. Be sure to remove any stems or ribs.
2. Place the tofu on a paper towel-lined plate and blot to remove the extra moisture.
3. Set a big nonstick skillet over medium-high heat and place the oil. Once the oil is warm, add the tofu and crumble it to cook, stirring often. Wait for approximately 5 minutes or until the tofu turns golden brown. Remove from the heat and set to the side.
4. Mix well using a spatula the liquid ingredients, except the oil, and add the lime zest.
5. Add the sauce to the skillet and combine.
6. Place the cabbage leaves on the plates and spoon the tofu mixture into the center, topping it with cilantro, cucumber, and pear.

Cinnamon Granola

Total Prep & Cooking Time: 25 min

Yields: 4 Servings

Nutrition Facts: Calories: 175 | Carbohydrates: 11 g | Proteins: 6 g | Fats: 17 g

Ingredients:

1 ½ t. cinnamon, ground

4 tbsp. maple syrup

1/5 oz. nuts

1 tbsp. chia seeds

5 tbsp. of the following:
- coconut flakes, unsweetened
- flaxseed meal

Follow these simple steps:

1. Bring the oven to 350 heat setting.
2. In a medium mixing bowl, combine the flaxseed, coconut, chia seed, nuts, and maple syrup. Mix well until combined.
3. Line a cookie sheet with parchment and spread the mixture in a single layer on the cookie sheet.
4. Across the top, sprinkle the cinnamon.
5. Place the cookie sheet in the oven, and wait for 20 minutes, approximately.
6. Once done, take it out and allow the granola to cool while still on the sheet.
7. Once cool, crumble to your desired liking and enjoy.

Chocolate Granola

Total Prep & Cooking Time: 60 min

Yields: 12 Servings

Nutrition Facts: Calories: 302 | Carbohydrates: 5.6 g | Proteins: 9.7 g | Fats: 24.8 g

Ingredients:

¼ t. sea salt

¼ c. of the following:
- hot water
- cocoa powder

1/3 c. of the following:
- coconut oil
- maple syrup, sugar-free

½ c. of the following:
- almond butter
- almond flour
- cashews, chopped

1 c. mixed seeds (flaxseed, sesame, sunflower, pumpkin)

2 c. coconut, flaked

2/3 c. almonds, flaked

Follow these simple steps:

1. Bring the oven to 300 heat setting.

2. In a little bowl, mix cocoa and hot water to form a thick paste.
3. Next, add to the little bowl the coconut oil, maple syrup, nut butter, and salt; mix until combined thoroughly.
4. In a big bowl, mix the almond meal, coconut flakes, seeds, and nuts.
5. Transfer the chocolate mixture to the big bowl and combine well.
6. Using a parchment-lined cookie sheet, spread out the granola mixture.
7. Bake for 40 minutes or until firm.
8. Allow to completely cool on the parchment.
9. Once cool, crumble to your desired liking and enjoy.

Radish Chips

Total Prep & Cooking Time: 1 hr. 40 min

Yields: 4 Servings

Nutrition Facts: Calories: 70 | Carbohydrates: 2.2 g | Proteins: 0.4 g | Fats: 7.1 g

Ingredients:

2 tbsp. olive oil (best if extra virgin)

16 oz. radishes

½ t. of the following:

- Black pepper, ground
- Salt

Follow these simple steps:

1. Bring the oven to 400 heat setting.
2. Using a mandolin, slice the radishes into 1/8th-inch slices.
3. Once sliced, use a paper towel to remove the excess moisture from the radishes by blotting the tops.
4. Prepare two cookie sheets with parchment paper, and spread the zucchini out into a single layer.
5. Add the seasonings in a bowl, with the olive oil. Whisk well and then brush each radish with this mixture, coating evenly and generously.
6. Bake for 10 minutes and then flip

7. Check every 5 minutes; once the radish is crispy, remove from the oven and serve.

Asparagus Fries

Total Prep & Cooking Time: 1 hr. 35 min

Yields: 4 Servings

Nutrition Facts: Calories: 183 | Carbohydrates: 10 g | Proteins: 8 g | Fats: 14 g

Ingredients:

2 tbsp. nutritional yeast

1 c. almond meal

1 t. of the following:
- maple syrup
- smoked paprika
- Himalayan pink salt

½ t. black pepper, ground

1 t. extra virgin olive oil

1 bunch asparagus

Follow these simple steps:

1. Set the oven to 400.

2. Prepare the asparagus by washing and cutting into equal halves.
3. In a big bowl, place the asparagus, add olive oil to the top, and toss to coat.
4. Add to the bowl the syrup, paprika, pepper, and salt and toss to coat.
5. In a medium, shallow bowl, mix the almond meal and nutritional yeast.
6. Line a cookie sheet with parchment paper and set to the side
7. Individually add each asparagus piece to the bowl, coating with your crumb mixture.
8. Place the asparagus on a lined cookie sheet; be sure not to overlap them.
9. Bake for 20 minutes or until brown.
10. Remove from the oven and serve.

Chapter 7: Sauces & Dips

Keto-Vegan Ketchup

Total Prep & Cooking Time: 35 min.

Yields: 12 Servings

Nutrition Facts: Calories: 13 | Carbohydrates: 2 g | Proteins: 0 g | Fats: 0 g

Ingredients:

1/8 t of the following:
- mustard powder
- cloves, ground

¼ t. paprika

½ t. garlic powder

¾ t. onion powder

1 t. sea salt

3 tbsp. apple cider vinegar

¼ c. powdered monk fruit

1 c. water

6 oz. tomato paste

Follow these simple steps:

1. In a little saucepan, whisk together all the ingredients.
2. Cover the pan and bring to low heat and simmer for 30 minutes, stirring occasionally.
3. Once reduced, add to the blender and puree until it's a smooth consistency.
4. Enjoy.

Avocado Hummus

Total Prep & Cooking Time: 5 min.

Yields: 6 Servings

Nutrition Facts: Calories: 310 | Carbohydrates: 26 g | Proteins: 8 g | Fats: 20 g

Ingredients:

1 tbsp. cilantro, finely chopped

1/8 t. cumin

1 clove garlic

3 tbsp. lime juice

1 ½ tbsp. of the following:
- tahini
- olive oil

2 avocados, medium cored & peeled

15 oz. chickpeas, drained

Salt and pepper to taste

Follow these simple steps:

1. In a food processor, add garlic, lime juice, tahini, olive oil, and chickpeas and pulse until combined.
2. Add cumin and avocados and blend until smooth consistency approximately 2 minutes.
3. Add salt and pepper to taste.

4. Enjoy.

Guacamole

Total Prep & Cooking Time: 5 min.

Yields: 6 Servings

Nutrition Facts: Calories: 127 | Carbohydrates: 9.3 g | Proteins: 2.4 g | Fats: 10.2 g

Ingredients:

3 tbsp. of the following:
- tomato, diced
- onion, diced

2 tbsp. of the following:
- cilantro, chopped
- jalapeno juice

¼ t. garlic powder

½ t. salt

½ lime, squeezed

2 big avocados

1 jalapeno, diced

Follow these simple steps:

1. Using a molcajete, crush the diced jalapenos until soft.
2. Add the avocados to the molcajete.
3. Squeeze the lime juice from ½ of the lime on top of the avocados.
4. Add the jalapeno juice, garlic, and salt and mix until smooth.
5. Once smooth, add in the onion, cilantro, and tomato and stir to incorporate.
6. Enjoy.

Keto-Vegan Mayo

Total Prep & Cooking Time: 5 min.

Yields: 6 Servings

Nutrition Facts: Calories: 160.4 | Carbohydrates: 0.2 g | Proteins: 0 g | Fats: 18 g

Ingredients:

½ c. of the following:
- extra virgin olive oil
- almond milk, unsweetened

¼ t. xanthan gum

Pinch of white pepper, ground

Pinch of Himalayan salt

1 t. Dijon mustard

2 t. apple cider vinegar

Follow these simple steps:

1. In a blender, place milk, pepper salt, mustard, and vinegar.
2. Turn the blender to high speed and slowly add xanthan then the olive oil.
3. Remove from the blender and allow cooling for 2 hours in the refrigerator.
4. During cooling, the mixture will thicken.

Peanut Sauce

Total Prep & Cooking Time: 10 min.

Yields: 4 Servings

Nutrition Facts: Calories: 151 | Carbohydrates: 4 g | Proteins: 4 g | Fats: 13 g

Ingredients:

½ t. Thai red curry paste

1 t. of the following:
- coconut oil
- soy Sauce
- chili garlic sauce

1 tbsp. sweetener of your choice

1/3 c. coconut milk

1.4 c. peanut butter, smooth

Follow these simple steps:

1. Using a microwave-safe dish, add the peanut butter and heat for about 30 seconds.
2. Whisk into the peanut butter, the soy sauce, sweetener, and chili garlic then set to the side.
3. Warm a little saucepan over medium heat and add oil.
4. Cook the Thai red curry paste until fragrant then add to a microwave-safe bowl.

5. Continuously stir the peanut mixture as you add the coconut milk. Stir until well-combined.
6. Enjoy at room temperature or warmed

Pistachio Dip

Total Prep & Cooking Time: 10 min.
Yields: 8 Servings
Nutrition Facts: Calories: 88 | Carbohydrates: 9 g | Proteins: 2.5 g | Fats: 3 g

Ingredients:

2 tbsp. lemon juice
1 t. extra virgin olive oil
2 tbsp. of the following:
- tahini
- parsley, chopped

2 cloves of garlic
½ c. pistachios shelled
15 oz. garbanzo beans, save the liquid from the can
Salt and pepper to taste

Follow these simple steps:

1. Using a food processor, add pistachios, pepper, sea salt, lemon juice, olive oil, tahini, parsley, garlic, and garbanzo beans. Pulse until mixed.
2. Using the liquid from the garbanzo beans, add to the dip while slowly blending until it reaches your desired consistency.
3. Enjoy at room temperature or warmed.

Smokey Tomato Jam

Total Prep & Cooking Time: 45 min.

Yields: 1 Cup

Nutrition Facts: Calories: 26 | Carbohydrates: 5.3 g | Proteins: 1.1 g | Fats: 0.6 g

Ingredients:

½ t. of the following:
- white wine vinegar
- salt

1/3 t. smoked paprika

Pinch Black pepper

¼ c. coconut sugar

2 pounds tomatoes

Follow these simple steps:

1. Over medium-high heat, bring a big pot of water to a boil.
2. Fill a big bowl with ice and water.
3. Carefully place the tomatoes into the boiling water for 1 minute and then remove, and immediately put into the ice water.
4. While tomatoes are in the ice water, peel them by hand and then transfer to a clean cutting surface.
5. Empty the pot of water.

6. Chop the tomatoes and place back into the pot; add in the coconut sugar and stir to combine.
7. Bring the pot back to medium heat and the tomatoes to a boil, cooking for 15 minutes.
8. Stir in the paprika, pepper, and salt and then bring the temperature down to the lowest setting. Let it cook until it becomes thick, which is approximately 10 minutes.
9. Remove it from the heat while continuing to stir; add in white wine vinegar.

Tasty Ranch Dressing/Dip

Total Prep & Cooking Time: 45 min.

Yields: 16 servings

Nutrition Facts: Calories: 93 | Carbohydrates: 0 g | Proteins: 0 g | Fats: 9 g

Ingredients:

½ c. soy milk, unsweetened

1 tbsp. dill, chopped

2 t. parsley, chopped

¼ t. black pepper

½ t. of the following:

- onion powder
- garlic powder

1 c. vegan mayonnaise

Follow these simple steps:

1. In a medium bowl, whisk all the ingredients together until smooth. If dressing is too thick, add ¼ tablespoon of soy milk at a time until the desired consistency.
2. Transfer to an airtight container or jar and refrigerate for 1 hour.
3. Serve over leafy greens or as a dip.

Chapter 8: Soups

These recipes are for those days when a hearty warm soup just hits the spot.

Goulash Soup

Total Prep & Cooking Time: 35 min.

Yields: 7 Servings

Nutrition Facts: Calories: 267 | Carbohydrates: 51.7 g | Proteins: 11.7 g | Fats: 3.1 g

Ingredients:

½ t. black pepper

14.5 oz. tomatoes, diced

8 little rutabagas, chopped into ½ inch chunks

¼ c. dry red wine

4 tbsp. paprika

1 t. salt

3 c. vegetable broth

6 cloves of garlic, minced

2 red bell peppers, chopped

2 c. onion, finely chopped

Follow these simple steps:

1. Prior to starting, ensure that you have all the vegetables washed and chopped. This recipe moves very quickly.
2. In a pot that is big enough for 7 servings, add the onion, garlic, and bell pepper after it has warmed in a medium heat setting.
3. Add to the pot ½ teaspoon of salt and 1 cup of the broth. Wait for it to bubble and then leave it cooking until the broth is gone. This usually just takes about 8 minutes.
4. Lower the temperature, and add the wine when most of the broth has evaporated. Add the paprika. Let the flavor seep in for a couple of minutes or a bit more.
5. Next, add the rest of the salt, pepper, tomatoes, rutabagas, and 1 ½ cup of broth. If you would like your dish to become saucier, add in the additional broth. Cook for 20 minutes or until the rutabaga is tender.
6. Serve and enjoy!

Celery Dill Soup

Total Prep & Cooking Time: 35 min.

Yields: 4 Servings

Nutrition Facts: Calories: 176 | Carbohydrates: 30.2 g | Proteins: 5.6 g | Fats: 13.6 g

Ingredients:

3 t. olive oil

½ c. pickle juice

½ onion, chopped

½ t. xanthan gum

¼ c dill pickle, finely chopped

1 stalk celery, chopped

¼ c. vegetable broth

1 t. of the following:
- parsley
- garlic, minced

1 tbsp. ghee

½ c. vegan bacon, crumbled

Follow these simple steps:

1. Before beginning, ensure you have chopped all vegetables.
2. In a big saucepan, melt ghee and garlic.

3. Add in the chopped pickles, onion, celery, and parsley and sauté for 5 minutes.
4. Next, add vegetable broth and pickle juice and bring to a boil.
5. In a little bowl, whisk together xanthan gum and olive oil then pour into the soup.
6. Continue to stir the soup frequently as it thickens.
7. Once thick, add crumbled bacon and serve.

Broccoli Fennel Soup

Total Prep & Cooking Time: 35 min.

Yields: 4 Servings

Nutrition Facts: Calories: 242 | Carbohydrates: 23.2 g | Proteins: 7.6 g | Fats: 15.4 g

Ingredients:

2 ½ c. kale

2 tbsp. lemon juice

3 c. water

½ c. cashews

1 medium onion, chopped

5 cloves garlic, minced

2 tbsp. olive oil

2 c. fennel, chopped

4 c. broccoli florets

Follow these simple steps:

1. Bring the oven to 400 heat setting.
2. Prepare a cookie sheet by lining it with paper.
3. Spread the florets and fennel on the cookie sheet; be careful not to overlap them and drizzle with 1 tablespoon of olive oil.
4. Place in the oven and roast for 10 minutes then flip and

roast for another 10 minutes.
5. While it is roasting, bring a heat a saucepan over medium-low heat.
6. Add in the remaining olive oil, and sauté the garlic for about 3 minutes; add in the onion and sauté for an additional 3 minutes.
7. After broccoli and fennel are finished roasting, add to the pan with the onion and garlic; mix thoroughly.
8. Finally, add the kale, lemon juice, water, and cashews. Simmer this for approximately 5 minutes.
9. Remove it from the stove and then blend using a machine you prefer, as long as it gets smooth.
10. Dust some salt and pepper or not, if you don't like additional salt. Serve.

Broccoli and Cauliflower Soup

Total Prep & Cooking Time: 35 min.

Yields: 8 Servings

Nutrition Facts: Calories: 204 | Carbohydrates: 14.7 g | Proteins: 9.5 g | Fats: 13.6 g

Ingredients:

1 tbsp. lemon juice

1 ½ t. salt

1/3 c. nutritional yeast

1 c. almond milk, unsweetened

4 c. vegetable broth

¼ c. almond flour

4 c. cauliflower, finely chopped

4 c. broccoli, finely chopped

2 carrots, diced

2 cloves garlic, minced

1 onion, chopped

2 tbsp. extra virgin olive oil

Follow these simple steps:

1. Pour some olive oil to a big-enough saucepan that has warmed using the medium heat setting.
2. Sauté for more than a couple of minutes the garlic, onion, and seasonings.
3. Add the chopped veggies (carrots, cauliflower, and broccoli) and sauté for another 5 minutes.
4. Next, add in the flour and stir to combine.
5. Once combined, add in the nutritional yeast, milk, and broth and then wait for it to boil just before turning the heat setting to medium-low.
6. While covered, let it simmer for about a quarter of an hour or less. Stir once in a while as you wait.
7. Remove from the heat and add in lemon juice. Using a hand blender, blend the soup contents until your desired level of chunkiness.
8. Dust with some salt and pepper to your taste and serve.

Keto-Vegan Chili

Total Prep & Cooking Time: 41 min.

Yields: 6 Servings

Nutrition Facts: Calories: 294 | Carbohydrates: 17.1 g | Proteins: 10.6 g | Fats: 23.7 g

Ingredients:

1 tbsp. cocoa powder, unsweetened

1 c. raw walnuts

16 oz. tofu, extra firm

½ c. coconut milk

3 c. water

15 oz. diced tomatoes

1 ½ tbsp. tomato paste

8 oz. cremini mushrooms

2 zucchini, diced

2 green bell peppers, diced

2 chipotle peppers in adobo sauce, minced

1 ½ t. paprika

4 t. cumin

2 t. chili powder

1 ½ t. cinnamon, ground

2 cloves garlic

5 stalks celery, diced

2 tbsp. extra virgin olive oil

Salt and pepper to taste

Follow these simple steps:

1. Prepare the tofu by taking it out of the package and blotting with a paper towel until most of the moisture is gone.
2. Bring a skillet to medium heat; crumble the tofu and cook until browned.
3. In a big saucepan, heat the olive oil under medium heat, add celery, and cook for 4 minutes.
4. Add the celery, paprika, cumin, chili powder, cinnamon, and garlic and sauté for 2 minutes.
5. Next, add the mushrooms, zucchini, and bell peppers and cook for approximately 5 minutes.
6. In the big saucepan add cocoa powder, walnuts, tofu, coconut milk, water, tomatoes, tomato paste, and chipotle and simmer for 20-25 minutes or until thick.
7. Dust with some salt and pepper according to preference.

Creamy Avocado Soup

Total Prep & Cooking Time: 46 min.

Yields: 3 Servings

Nutrition Facts: Calories: 226.3 | Carbohydrates: 5.8 g | Proteins: 3.3 g | Fats: 20 g

Ingredients:

1/3 c. cilantro

1/8 t. black pepper

¼ t. salt

1 lime, juiced

1/3 c. coconut milk

½ c. vegetable stock

¼ c. cucumber

2 cloves garlic

2 avocados

Follow these simple steps:

1. In a blender, add avocado, cucumber, lime juice, cilantro, coconut milk, vegetable stock, and garlic.
2. Blend until completely smooth. If you prefer a thinner soup, add additional vegetable stock.
3. Transfer to a big serving bowl and refrigerate for 30 minutes.

4. Dust some salt and pepper to your taste and serve.

Red Onion Soup

Total Prep & Cooking Time: 20 min.

Yields: 2 Servings

Nutrition Facts: Calories: 521 | Carbohydrates: 15.1 g | Proteins: 11.9 g | Fats: 48.4 g

Ingredients:

2 t. pesto

4 tbsp. walnuts

5 tbsp. olive oil

2 tbsp. lemon juice

2 ½ c. vegetable broth

2 cloves garlic, minced

2 red onions

1 t. oregano

Follow these simple steps:

1. Begin by cutting the onion into thin rings and set to the side.
2. In a big pot, add garlic and onions and sauté for 5 minutes.

3. Add in the vegetable broth, oregano, and lemon juice and bring to a simmer for approximately 10 minutes, stirring occasionally.
4. In a skillet, add some olive oil and walnuts; fry for 3 minutes until toasted. Then add to the soup.
5. Finally, add the rest of the seasoning, including the pesto, according to your preference. Serve piping hot.

Thai Pumpkin Soup

Total Prep & Cooking Time: 20 min.

Yields: 4 Servings

Nutrition Facts: Calories: 361 | Carbohydrates: 24.9 g | Proteins: 9.4 g | Fats: 27 g

Ingredients:

1 red chili pepper sliced

13.5 oz. coconut milk

30 oz. pumpkin puree, can

4 c. vegetable broth

2 tbsp. red curry paste

Follow these simple steps:

1. Sit a big saucepan over medium heat; cook the curry paste for about 60 seconds or until the kitchen smells like curry heaven.
2. Pour in the broth, including the pumpkin, stirring to integrate the flavors.
3. Under the same heat setting, wait for the soup to bubble slightly. That's your cue to add the coconut milk. When combined, cook for about 3 minutes.
4. Finally, add to individual bowls and garnish with sliced red chili pepper. Enjoy hot.

Zucchini Basil Soup

Total Prep & Cooking Time: 20 min.

Yields: 4 Servings

Nutrition Facts: Calories: 200 | Carbohydrates: 18 g | Proteins: 3 g | Fats: 14.3 g

Ingredients:

1 c. basil leaves

¾ t. salt

2 c. water

4 cloves garlic

1 ½ pound sliced zucchini

½ t. apple cider vinegar

2 tbsp. olive oil

1 onion, diced

Follow these simple steps:

1. Place a medium-size saucepan over medium-high heat.
2. Sauté the onions and garlic for 2 minutes.
3. Add zucchini and water to the pan and bring to a simmer, cover, and cook for 15 minutes, stirring occasionally.
4. Remove from the heat, and using a hand blender, carefully add in the basil and blend until smooth.
5. Once smooth, add in vinegar and salt and pepper to taste.

6. Finally, add to individual bowls and enjoy.

Chapter 9: Smoothies

Chocolate Smoothie

Total Prep & Cooking Time: 5 min.

Yields: 2 Servings

Nutrition Facts: Calories: 147 | Carbohydrates: 8.2 g | Proteins: 4 g | Fats: 13.4 g

Ingredients:

¼ c. almond butter

¼ c. cocoa powder, unsweetened

½ c. coconut milk, canned

1 c. almond milk, unsweetened

Follow these simple steps:

1. Before making the smoothie, freeze the almond milk into cubes using an ice cube tray. This would take a few hours, so prepare it ahead.
2. Blend everything using your preferred machine until it reaches your desired thickness.
3. Serve immediately and enjoy!

Chocolate Mint Smoothie

Total Prep & Cooking Time: 5 min.

Yields: 1 Serving

Nutrition Facts: Calories: 401 | Carbohydrates: 6.3 g | Proteins: 5 g | Fats: 40.3 g

Ingredients:

2 tbsp. sweetener of your choice

2 drops mint extract

1 tbsp. cocoa powder

½ avocado, medium

¼ c. coconut milk

1 c. almond milk, unsweetened

Follow these simple steps:

1. In a high-speed blender, add all the ingredients and blend until smooth.
2. Add two to four ice cubes and blend.
3. Serve immediately and enjoy!

Cinnamon Roll Smoothie

Total Prep & Cooking Time: 2 min.

Yields: 1 Serving

Nutrition Facts: Calories: 507 | Carbohydrates: 17 g | Proteins: 33.3 g | Fats: 34.9 g

Ingredients:

1 t. cinnamon

1 scoop vanilla protein powder

½ c. of the following:
- almond milk, unsweetened
- coconut milk

Sweetener of your choice

Follow these simple steps:
1. In a high-speed blender, add all the ingredients and blend.
2. Add two to four ice cubes and blend until smooth.
3. Serve immediately and enjoy!

Coconut Smoothie

Total Prep & Cooking Time: 2 min.

Yields: 2 Servings

Nutrition Facts: Calories: 584 | Carbohydrates: 22.5 g | Proteins: 8.3 g | Fats: 55.5 g

Ingredients:

1 t. chia seeds

1/8 c. almonds, soaked

1 c. coconut milk

1 avocado

Follow these simple steps:
1. In a high-speed blender, add all the ingredients and blend until smooth.
2. Add your desired number of ice cubes, depending on your favored consistency, of course, and blend again.
3. Serve immediately and enjoy!

Maca Almond Smoothie

Total Prep & Cooking Time: 5 min.

Yields: 2 Servings

Nutrition Facts: Calories: 758 | Carbohydrates: 28.6 g | Proteins: 9.3 g | Fats: 72.3 g

Ingredients:

½ t. vanilla extract

1 scoop maca powder

1 tbsp. almond butter

1 c. almond milk, unsweetened

2 avocados

Follow these simple steps:
1. In a high-speed blender, add all the ingredients and blend until smooth.
2. Serve immediately and enjoy!

Blueberry Smoothie

Total Prep & Cooking Time: 5 min.

Yields: 1 Serving

Nutrition Facts: Calories: 401 | Carbohydrates: 6.3 g | Proteins: 5 g | Fats: 40.3 g

Ingredients:

¼ c. pumpkin seeds shelled unsalted

3 c. blueberries, frozen

2 avocados, peeled and halved

1 c. almond milk

Follow these simple steps:

1. In a high-speed blender, add all the ingredients and blend until smooth.
2. Add two to four ice cubes and blend until smooth.
3. Serve immediately and enjoy!

Nutty Protein Shake

Total Prep & Cooking Time: 5 min.

Yields: 1 Serving

Nutrition Facts: Calories: 694 | Carbohydrates: 30.8 g | Proteins: 40.8 g | Fats: 52 g

Ingredients:

¼ avocado

2 tbsp. powdered peanut butter

1 tbsp. of the following:
- Cocoa powder
- Peanut butter

1 scoop protein powder

½ c. almond milk

Follow these simple steps:
1. In a high-speed blender, add all the ingredients and blend until smooth.
2. Add two to four ice cubes and blend again.
3. Serve immediately and enjoy!

Cinnamon Pear Smoothie

Total Prep & Cooking Time: 2 min.

Yields: 1 Serving

Nutrition Facts: Calories: 653 | Carbohydrates: 75.2 g | Proteins: 28.4 g | Fats: 32.2 g

Ingredients:

1 t. cinnamon

1 scoop vanilla protein powder

½ c. of the following:
- Almond milk, unsweetened
- Coconut Milk

2 pears, cores removed

Sweetener of your choice

Follow these simple steps:
1. In a high-speed blender, add all the ingredients and blend.
2. Add two or more ice cubes and blend again.
3. Serve immediately and enjoy!

Vanilla Milkshake

Total Prep & Cooking Time: 5 min.

Yields: 4 Servings

Nutrition Facts: Calories: 125 | Carbohydrates: 6.8 g | Proteins: 1.2 g | Fats: 11.5 g

Ingredients:

2 c. ice cubes

2 t. vanilla extract

6 tbsp. powdered erythritol

1 c. cream of dairy-free

½ c. coconut milk

Follow these simple steps:
1. In a high-speed blender, add all the ingredients and blend.
2. Add ice cubes and blend until smooth.
3. Serve immediately and enjoy!

Raspberry Protein Shake

Total Prep & Cooking Time: 5 min.

Yields: 1 Serving

Nutrition Facts: Calories: 756 | Carbohydrates: 80.1 g | Proteins: 27.6 g | Fats: 40.7 g

Ingredients:

¼ avocado

1 c. raspberries, frozen

1 scoop protein powder

½ c. almond milk

Ice cubes

Follow these simple steps:
1. In a high-speed blender add all the ingredients and blend until lumps of fruit disappear.
2. Add two to four ice cubes and blend to your desired consistency.
3. Serve immediately and enjoy!

Raspberry Almond Smoothie

Total Prep & Cooking Time: 5 min.

Yields: 1 Serving

Nutrition Facts: Calories: 449 | Carbohydrates: 26 g | Proteins: 14 g | Fats: 35 g

Ingredients:

10 Almonds, finely chopped

3 tbsp. almond butter

1 c. almond milk

1 c. Raspberries, frozen

Follow these simple steps:
1. In a high-speed blender, add all the ingredients and blend until smooth.
2. Serve immediately and enjoy!

Chapter 10: Desserts

Keto Chocolate Brownies

Total Prep & Cooking Time: 30 min.

Yields: 16 Servings

Nutrition Facts: Calories: 131 | Carbohydrates: 12.3 g | Proteins: 1.8 g | Fats: 8.8 g

Ingredients:

¼ t. of the following:
- salt
- baking soda

½ c. of the following:
- sweetener of your choice
- coconut flour

- vegetable oil
- water

¼ c. of the following:

- cocoa powder
- almond milk yogurt

1 tbsp. ground flax

1 t. vanilla extract

Follow these simple steps:

1. Bring the oven to 350 heat setting.
2. Mix the ground flax, vanilla, yogurt, oil, and water; set to the side for 10 minutes.
3. Line an oven-safe 8x8 baking dish with parchment paper.
4. After 10 minutes have passed, add coconut flour, cocoa powder, sweetener, baking soda, and salt.
5. Bake for 15 minutes; make sure that you placed it in the center. When they come out, they will look underdone.
6. Place in the refrigerator and let them firm up overnight.

Chocolate Fat Bomb

Total Prep & Cooking Time: 5 min.

Yields: 14 Servings

Nutrition Facts: Calories: 84 | Carbohydrates: 2.6 g | Proteins: 2 g | Fats: 8.2 g

Ingredients:

1 tbsp. liquid sweetener of your choice.

¼ c. of the following:
- coconut oil, melted
- cocoa powder

½ c. almond butter

Follow these simple steps:

1. Mix the ingredients in a medium bowl until smooth. Pour into the candy molds or ice cube trays.
2. Put in the freezer to set.
3. Store in freezer.

Vanilla Cheesecake

Total Prep & Cooking Time: 3 hr. 20 min.

Yields: 10 Servings

Nutrition Facts: Calories: 300 | Carbohydrates: 7.7 g | Proteins: 7.1 g | Fats: 28.3 g

Ingredients:

1 tbsp. vanilla extract,
2 ½ tbsp. lemon juice
½ c. coconut oil
1/8 t. stevia powder
6 tbsp. coconut milk
1 ½ c. blanched almonds soaked

Crust:

2 tbsp. coconut oil
1 ½ c. almonds

Follow these simple steps:

For the Crust:

1. In a food processor, add the almonds and coconut oil and pulse until crumbles start to form.

2. Line a 7-inch springform pan with parchment paper and firmly press the crust into the bottom.

For the Sauce:

3. Bring a saucepan of water to a boil and soak the almonds for 2 hours. Drain and shake to dry.
4. Next, add the almonds to the food processor and blend until completely smooth.
5. Add vanilla, lemon, coconut oil, stevia, and coconut milk and blend until smooth.
6. Pour over the crust and freeze overnight or for a minimum of 3 hours.
7. Serve and enjoy.

Chocolate Mousse

Total Prep & Cooking Time: 5 min.

Yields: 2 Servings

Nutrition Facts: Calories: 420| Carbohydrates: 13.5 g | Proteins: 6.2 g | Fats: 42.9 g

Ingredients:

6 drops liquid stevia extract

½ t. cinnamon

3 tbsp. cocoa powder, unsweetened

1 c. coconut milk

Follow these simple steps:

1. On the day before, place the coconut milk into the refrigerator overnight.

2. Remove the coconut milk from the refrigerator; it should be very thick.
3. Whisk in cocoa powder with an electric mixer.
4. Add stevia and cinnamon and whip until combined.
5. Place in individual bowls and serve and enjoy.

Avocado Chocolate Mousse

Total Prep & Cooking Time: 3 hr. 20 min.

Yields: 4 Servings

Nutrition Facts: Calories: 343 | Carbohydrates: 12 g | Proteins: 3.3 g | Fats: 33.9 g

Ingredients:

2 pinches sea salt

4 tbsp. sweetener of your choice

1 c. almond milk, unsweetened

2 avocados, peeled and pitted

Follow these simple steps:

1. Blend everything using a machine of your choice, as long as the consistency becomes smooth for a mousse. If too thick, add some more coconut milk, ¼ teaspoon at a time.
2. Serve and enjoy.

Coconut Fat Bombs

Total Prep & Cooking Time: 1 hr. 5 min.

Yields: 4 Servings

Nutrition Facts: Calories: 89.1 | Carbohydrates: 0.87 g | Proteins: 0.33 g | Fats: 9.7 g

Ingredients:

20 drops liquid stevia
1 c. coconut flakes, unsweetened
¾ c. coconut oil
1 can coconut milk

Follow these simple steps:

1. In a big microwave-safe mixing bowl, add coconut oil and warm on low power for 20 seconds to melt.
2. Whisk in coconut milk and stevia into the oil.
3. Add coconut flakes; combine well.
4. Pour into candy molds or ice cube trays and freeze for 1 hour.
5. Serve and enjoy.

Coconut Cupcakes

Total Prep & Cooking Time: 1 hr. 5 min.

Yields: 18 Servings

Nutrition Facts: Calories: 202 | Carbohydrates: 15.6 g | Proteins: 3.3 g | Fats: 15.8 g

Ingredients:

1 tbsp. vanilla

1 t. baking soda

1 c. erythritol

4 t. baking powder

1 ¼ c. coconut milk

¾ c. coconut flour

14 tbsp. arrowroot powder

2 c. almond meal

½ c. coconut oil

Whipped Cream:

1 t. vanilla

¼ c. erythritol

2 13.5 oz. cans full-fat coconut milk, refrigerated overnight

Follow these simple steps:

1. Prepare a muffin tin with muffin liners and bring the oven to 350 heat setting.
2. In a big mixing bowl, add all the ingredients and beat on medium-high speed until it turns to a batter-like consistency. If too dry, add ¼ teaspoon of water at a time.
3. Fill the cupcake cups with the batter, three-quarters full.
4. Bake for 20 minutes or until the cupcakes are firm.
5. Place in the refrigerator to cool.
6. While cupcakes are cooling, make the whipped cream.
7. Remove the coconut milk from the fridge and pour the clear coconut water from the milk.
8. In a big mixing bowl, add the vanilla and erythritol; beat until fluffy.
9. Ice the cupcakes and serve.
10. Serve and enjoy.

Pumpkin Truffles

Total Prep & Cooking Time: 15 min.

Yields: 12 Servings

Nutrition Facts: Calories: 66 | Carbohydrates: 10 g | Proteins: 1 g | Fats: 2 g

Ingredients:

1 t. cinnamon

2 tbsp. coconut sugar

3 tbsp. coconut flour

½ c. almond flour

1 t. pumpkin pie spice

¼ t. salt

½ t. vanilla extract

¼ c. maple syrup

1 c. pumpkin puree

Follow these simple steps:

1. Bring a saucepan to medium heat and add pumpkin puree, syrup, salt, and pumpkin pie spice, stirring constantly until thickened about 5 minutes.
2. Once thick, add in vanilla and continue to stir for an additional minute.
3. Remove from the heat and allow to cool.

4. Once cool, mix in the coconut and almond flour. Then put in the refrigerator to chill for 10 minutes.
5. Remove from the fridge and mix again. If the dough is too sticky, add in 1 tablespoon of almond flour until you can form a ball with the dough.
6. Form 12 balls using your hands with the dough.
7. In a little bowl, combine coconut sugar and cinnamon.
8. Roll each ball into the cinnamon-sugar mixture.
9. Serve and enjoy.

Raspberry Truffles

Total Prep & Cooking Time: 15 min.

Yields: 36 Servings

Nutrition Facts: Calories: 39 | Carbohydrates: 3.8 g | Proteins: 0.6 g | Fats: 2.6 g

Ingredients:

2 tbsp. cocoa powder, unsweetened

6 oz. of the following:

- fresh raspberries, dry
- chocolate, bittersweet, finely chopped
- coconut milk, full-fat

Follow these simple steps:

1. Prepare a cookie sheet with parchment paper and set to the side.
2. Warm a saucepan over medium heat, and add coconut milk.
3. Remove from the heat and add the chocolate with a rubber spatula, stirring to melt the chocolate
4. Once smooth, add the raspberries, 5-8 at a time. Stir to coat.
5. Using two forks, remove the raspberries from the chocolate sauce, allowing the excess sauce to drop back

into the pan. Repeat this step until you have coated all raspberries.
6. Place the raspberries in the refrigerator for 1 hour or until firm.
7. In a shallow bowl with a lid, add the cocoa powder.
8. Once truffles are firm, place 5 to 8 truffles in the bowl and shake to coat with cocoa powder.
9. Return to the refrigerator until ready to serve.

Strawberry Ice Cream

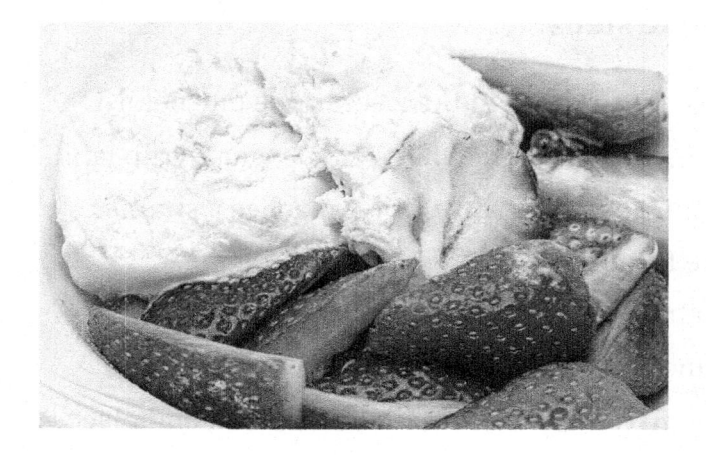

Total Prep & Cooking Time: 7 hr. 60 min.

Yields: 8 Servings

Nutrition Facts: Calories: 273 | Carbohydrates: 23.9 g | Proteins: 1.4 g | Fats: 19.4 g

Ingredients:

½ t. salt

1 tbsp. strawberry extract

1 c. strawberry puree

¼ c. maple syrup

½ c. sweetener of your choice

14 oz. coconut milk

14 oz. coconut cream

You will need an ice cream maker for this recipe.

Follow these simple steps:

1. Place your ice cream bowl in the freezer one day before.
2. In a saucepan, pour in the coconut milk, sugar, syrup, and coconut cream, gently stirring until it reaches a simmer. Then remove from the heat.
3. Add in salt, strawberry extract, and strawberry puree then blend with an immersion blender until smooth.
4. Transfer the mixture into a container with a lid and place in the freezer to chill for 30 minutes.
5. Following the directions on your ice cream maker, churn the mixture for about 20-40 minutes until a soft-serve consistency is reached.
6. Transfer to a loaf pan and place in the freezer for approximately 6 hours.
7. Scoop and serve.

Pistachio Gelato

Total Prep & Cooking Time: 7 hr. 60 min.

Yields: 4 Servings

Nutrition Facts: Calories: 345 | Carbohydrates: 38.8 g | Proteins: 6.5 g | Fats: 19.8 g

Ingredients:

½ t. almond extract

1 c. of the following:
- Medjool dates
- pistachios, unsalted, shells removed

1 big avocado

2 ½ c. cashew milk

Follow these simple steps:

1. In a blender, add almond extract, dates, pistachios, avocado, and milk and blend until smooth.
2. Once smooth, pour into a loaf pan, topping with chopped pistachios and freeze for 8 hours or overnight.
3. Remove from the freezer and allow to fall for 15 minutes before serving.
4. Scoop and serve.

Chocolate Chip Ice Cream

Total Prep & Cooking Time: 7 hr. 60 min.

Yields: 8 Servings

Nutrition Facts: Calories: 429 | Carbohydrates: 48.2 g | Proteins: 3.3 g | Fats: 26.2 g

Ingredients:

½ t. salt

1 c. chocolate chips

¼ c. maple syrup

½ c. sweetener of your choice

14 oz. of the following:

- Coconut milk
- Coconut cream

You will need an ice cream maker for this recipe.

Follow these simple steps:

1. Place your ice cream bowl in the freezer on the day before.
2. In a saucepan, add coconut milk, sugar, syrup, and coconut cream, gently stirring until it reaches a simmer. Then remove from heat.
3. Add in salt and blend with an immersion blender until smooth.

4. Transfer mixture into a container with a lid and place in the freezer to chill for 15 minutes.
5. Remove from the freezer and fold in the chocolate chips. Place back in the freezer for an additional 15 minutes
6. Following the directions on your ice cream maker, churn the mixture for about 20-40 minutes until a soft-serve consistency is reached.
7. Transfer to a loaf pan and place in the freezer for approximately 6 hours.
8. Scoop and serve.

Cinnamon Vanilla Bites

Total Prep & Cooking Time: 60 min.

Yields: 15 Servings

Nutrition Facts: Calories: 194 | Carbohydrates: 8.9 g | Proteins: 11.9 g | Fats: 14.4 g

Ingredients:

2 tbsp. water

1 t. vanilla extract

1 tbsp. cinnamon

¼ c. of the following:
- vanilla vegan protein powder
- maple syrup

½ c. of the following:
- almonds, unsalted
- almond butter

¾ c hemp hearts

For coating:

1 t cinnamon + 1 tbsp. vanilla protein powder

Follow these simple steps:

1. In a food processor, add vanilla, cinnamon, protein powder, syrup, almonds, almond butter, and hemp hearts and blend until combined.
2. Add water, ½ tablespoon at a time, until the mixture begins to stick together and form a ball.
3. Using your hands, form 1 ½ inch balls.
4. In a shallow bowl with a lid, combine 1 teaspoon cinnamon and 2 tablespoons of protein powder.
5. Add a few balls at a time to the bowl and coat with the powder mixture.
6. Store in refrigerator and serve cool.

Berry Bites

Total Prep & Cooking Time: 60 min.

Yields: 13 Servings

Nutrition Facts: Calories: 75 | Carbohydrates: 2.8 g | Proteins: 0.8 g | Fats: 7.2 g

Ingredients:

Dash Himalayan pink salt

1/16 t. stevia

½ t. vanilla

½ c. blackberries

2/3 c. coconut butter

Follow these simple steps:

1. In a food processor, add coconut butter, blackberries, vanilla, stevia, and salt; blend until well combined.
2. Using your hands, form them into 1 ½-inch balls, and place them on parchment a paper on a flat dish.
3. Place the dish in the freezer for 15 minutes to set.
4. Store in refrigerator and serve cool.

Coconut Chocolate Balls

Total Prep & Cooking Time: 20 min.

Yields: 22 Servings

Nutrition Facts: Calories: 179 | Carbohydrates: 18.6 g | Proteins: 6 g | Fats: 10.2 g

Ingredients:

¼ c. of the following:
- coconut, unsweetened, finely shredded
- coconut oil, melted

16 oz. Medjool dates

1 1/3 c. hemp hearts

¼ t. sea salt, ground

2 tbsp. ground flaxseed

½ c. cocoa, unsweetened

¾ c. almonds, sliced

Follow these simple steps:

1. In a food processor, finely chop the almonds for 30 seconds.
2. Next, add in the hemp hearts, sea salt, flaxseed, and cocoa and blend for another 30 seconds.
3. Add in the coconut oil and dates; blend it for 2 minutes or until well-blended. If the mixture is not sticking together, add ¼ t. of coconut oil until sticky.
4. Using your hands, form them into 1 ½-inch balls.
5. Place on a paper-lined dish and store into the freezer for 15 minutes to set.
6. In a shallow bowl, place finely shredded coconut. Roll each ball into the coconut, pressing gently but firmly.
7. Store in the refrigerator and serve cool.

Espresso Cups

Total Prep & Cooking Time: 20 min.

Yields: 22 Servings

Nutrition Facts: Calories: 77 | Carbohydrates: 1 g | Proteins: 1 g | Fats: 8 g

Ingredients:

15 drops vanilla stevia

1 ½ tbsp. instant espresso powder

1 tbsp. coconut milk

2 tbsp. cocoa powder

1/3 c. of the following:
- coconut oil
- almond butter

Follow these simple steps:

1. In a saucepan over medium-low heat, melt the almond butter, coconut oil, coconut powder, coconut milk, espresso powder, and stevia. Stir frequently not to scorch.
2. Pour into the candy molds or ice cube trays and freeze for 30 minutes.
3. Store in the refrigerator and serve cool.

Conclusion

I hope you found your copy of *Keto-Vegan Cookbook for Beginners* helpful. I hope you found some sections informative and were provided lots of great new tools to help you live your keto-vegan lifestyle. I say "lifestyle" because the word diet is not really appropriate. If you want to find success in healthy living, it has to be a lifestyle choice, not simply a diet that will end at some given date in the future. Living on the keto-vegan lifestyle offers so many different physical and health benefits, along with the opportunity to expand your taste buds to different spices and cuisines you may have never considered.

The next step is to prepare that shopping list and head to the market. Be sure to pay attention to what might be seasonally prepared and when those ingredients are the freshest. The fresher the ingredients are, the better the dish. Always look for organic or naturally sourced produce to make sure you are getting top-quality freshness.

Before you know it, you will be the envy of the neighborhood with your delicious healthy meals and amazing desserts. Taking steps to better your health is a hard choice to make. Congratulations, you have done the hard part and have taken that first step to a better life. Using this book, you will not only have a variety of dishes to satisfy your taste buds, but you might also surprise your carnivore friends.

Index for the Recipes

Chapter 4: Breakfast Choices

Strawberry Porridge
Gingerbread Porridge
Overnight Strawberry Cheesecake Porridge
Blueberry Quinoa Porridge
Blueberry Chia Pudding
Almond Flour Muffins
Bulletproof Tea
Bulletproof Coffee
Coconut Pancakes
Flaxseed Pancakes
Berry and Nut Cereal
Peanut Butter Fudgy Brownies
Vanilla Golden Turmeric Cereal
Fudge Oatmeal
Raspberry Almond Smoothie
Vanilla Overnight Oats
Cinnamon Overnight Oats
Pumpkin Spice Overnight Oats
Smoothie Bowl
Eggy Surprise Scramble
Bagels
Cinnamon Roll Muffins

Chapter 5: Lunch & Dinner Favorites

Mushroom Steak
Spicy Grilled Tofu Steak
Piquillo Salsa Verde Steak
Butternut Squash Steak
Cauliflower Steak Kicking Corn
Pistachio Watermelon Steak
BBQ Ribs
Spicy Veggie Steaks With veggies
Tofu Seitan
Stuffed Zucchini
Roasted Butternut Squash With Chimichurri

Eggplant Pizza
Green Avocado Carbonara
Curried Tofu
Sesame Tofu and Eggplant
Tempeh Coconut Curry
Tempeh Tikka Masala
Caprice Casserole
Cheesy Brussel Sprout Bake
Tofu Noodle Bowl
Cashew Siam Salad
Cucumber Edamame Salad
Caesar Vegan Salad
Mushroom Lettuce Wraps

Chapter 6: Side Dishes & Snacks

Mixed Seed Crackers
Crispy Squash Chips
Paprika Nuts
Basil Zoodles and Olives
Roasted Beetroot Noodles
Turnip Fries
Lime and Chili Carrots Noodles
Pesto Zucchini Noodles

Cabbage Slaw
Zucchini Chips
Peanut Tofu Wrap
Cinnamon Granola
Chocolate Granola
Radish Chips
Asparagus Fries

Chapter 7: Sauces & Dips

Keto-Vegan Ketchup
Avocado Hummus
Guacamole
Keto-Vegan Mayo
Peanut Sauce
Pistachio Dip
Smokey Tomato Jam
Tasty Ranch Dressing/Dip

Chapter 8: Soups

Goulash Soup
Celery Dill Soup
Broccoli Fennel Soup
Broccoli and Cauliflower Soup

Keto-Vegan Chili
Creamy Avocado Soup
Red Onion Soup
Thai Pumpkin Soup
Zucchini Basil Soup

Chapter 9: Smoothies

Chocolate Smoothie
Chocolate Mint Smoothie
Cinnamon Roll Smoothie
Coconut Smoothie
Maca Almond Smoothie
Blueberry Smoothie
Nutty Protein Shake
Cinnamon Pear Smoothie
Vanilla Milkshake
Raspberry Protein Shake
Raspberry Almond Smoothie

Chapter 10 Deserts

Keto Chocolate Brownies
Chocolate Fat Bomb
Vanilla Cheesecake
Chocolate Mousse

Avocado Chocolate Mousse
Coconut Fat Bombs
Coconut Cupcakes
Pumpkin Truffles
Raspberry Truffles
Strawberry Ice Cream
Pistachio Gelato
Chocolate Chip Ice Cream
Cinnamon Vanilla Bites
Berry Bites
Coconut Chocolate Balls
Espresso Cups

Made in the USA
Monee, IL
02 January 2020